Life's Little Pleasures

Life's Little Pleasures

GEORGE HAMILTON
AND ALYSSE MINKOFF

GPG
GENERAL PUBLISHING GROUP, INC
LOS ANGELES

Publisher: W. Quay Hays
Editorial Director: Peter L. Hoffman
Designer: Dana Granoski

For information:

General Publishing Group, Inc.
2701 Ocean Park Blvd., Suite 140
Santa Monica, CA 90405

Library of Congress Cataloging-in-Publication Data

Hamilton, George, 1939–
Life's little pleasures / by George Hamilton and Alysse Minkoff :
p. cm.
ISBN 1-57544-086-5 (hardcover)
1. Hamilton, George, 1939– . 2. motion picture actors and actresses—United States—Biography. 3. Conduct of life.
I. Title.
PN2287.H178A3 1998
791.43'028'092—dc21
[B]
98-29268
CIP

Printed in the USA by RR Donnelley & Sons Company
10 9 8 7 6 5 4 3 2 1

General Publishing Group
Los Angeles

Table of Contents

Life's Little Pleasures

SOME THOUGHTS *on Pleasure*

A place of pleasure is one that is eternally yours. I'm not talking about the momentary thrill of landing a new job, or the joy of getting a new haircut, or the rush of driving a brand-new Ferrari. Those experiences, however amusing, are fleeting, and Pleasure is something much deeper than that. It's about feeling satisfied and content by oneself. It is usually an entirely internal phenomenon, independent of a set of external circumstances. Pleasure isn't necessarily about acquiring material possessions or achieving a certain status in life. It is about developing a long-standing connection with that tiny bubble of joy that resides in us all.

Let's face facts: If fame, power, and money were the keys to living a good life, we would not have witnessed an inordinate number of famous, powerful, and wealthy people destroy themselves over the years. And if fame, power, and money were the only yardsticks that mattered to me, I wouldn't be here today. Certainly my career has been considered dead in the water at least eight different times. After enduring a very public divorce, I am now on great terms with my former wife, Alana. Our son, Ashley, is doing well following a rough patch in his life. I've remained friends with most of the women with whom I have been romantically involved. And I am enjoying a new career as a cigar manufacturer and nightclub owner and restaurateur. All in all, not too bad. I just hope I don't sound like Shirley Temple.

I'm proud to say that looking back over the years, not only have I survived, but I have done so with a great deal of style—my own style. I have learned that the

This is me around the age of eight.

Of course I hadn't quite perfected my theory about the importance of a good haircut and the right clothes.

secret to happiness lies in creating my own game and playing by my own rules. Early on I set internal standards for happiness. I never measured success in terms of what was rung up at the box office or whose party I did or did not get invited to. Sure, people have laughed at my image, but I'm usually the first one to beat them to the punch. Let me tell you, it's been a long and interesting road from 1960's *Where the Boys Are* to 1990's *The Godfather Part III*. I've always had a great time, and that sense of fun is contagious.

What has kept me relatively sane through the ups and downs, the love affairs and the breakups, great wealth and just getting by, is my attitude. My image bespeaks a certain level of Pleasure, an aura of glamour and style, if you will. Occasionally a little wicked decadence, too. Pleasure is what I am all about, whether I'm running my cigar business or out on a date with a woman, whether I'm on a soundstage or in a boardroom. If I had believed the best or the worst of my press, I would have been out of the game a long time ago. My life is about Pleasure and leading a pleasurable life, regardless of what is going on outside of me.

Contrary to popular belief, true Pleasure is not something that anyone else can give you. Pleasure is about having a relationship with yourself: a deep, long-lasting, and passionate love affair with your own soul. And whatever road you choose to get to that place, the journey can be an amazing one. This book is meant to stimulate your imagination about the myriad ways, large and small, Pleasure can be added to your life. And enjoying the life you have is what it's all about, isn't it?

A pleasurable life isn't about filling your world with an ever-expanding array of the latest consumer goods, or props, as I call them. I am not of the philosophy that he who dies—or lives—with the most toys wins. Pleasure cannot be purchased, rented, or left to you in your great uncle's will. It isn't necessarily the props that matter here, but it is important to know when and where to use them; knowing how to touch your own soul, to access that place of Pleasure inside your own being and be happy there.

If you stop and think about it for a moment, a relationship with yourself is the only relationship in your life that is forever. Spouses come and go (although ex-wives are forever). Children, in spite of their best efforts to the contrary, eventually become independent and move on with their own lives. Friends drift in and out again. Even in the most romantic love affair, the music eventually fades. You are left with the one person you have spent most of your life trying to avoid: you. So, before you can bring even the most insignificant 'other' into your life, you should have a fairly sound grasp of the inner map of your own psyche. You should know what makes you happy, and you should be able to get there alone.

Sometimes places of pleasure can be incredibly personal, and the mere act of sharing it with another can diminish it. I'm not saying that you should grab your silver flask and cashmere blanket, and meditate on the side of some cliff, spending your days in solitary contemplation (although the idea does have its merits). We all have to live in the world. We must earn a living, relate to other people, place demands on others, and have people rely on us. But before you can have a solid relationship with anyone else, shouldn't you first have a good one with yourself? Leading a pleasurable life is all about knowing which buttons to push in your own life that can create a place of happiness for yourself. It's about taking yourself out of the mundane and delighting yourself, however fleeting. It's about being *in* the world yet not *of* it.

Life at the close of this millennium bombards us with information. We have voice mail and cellular telephones, e-mail and faxes, 150 channels on our satellite dishes. We live in an age in which everything is readily and instantly available to us. We don't browse through the quaint corner bookstore anymore; instead, we order books on the Internet. We don't board a train in California and spend a week crossing the country, acclimating leisurely to the time zones as the scenery changes; instead, we are treated like potential terrorists at the airport, interrogated by security. By the time we get to the gate, we might as well have walked all the way to New York. In our goal-oriented lives, elegance, grace, and style are elements that have been forsaken in favor of expedience. We have become greedy consumers instead of knowledgeable connoisseurs.

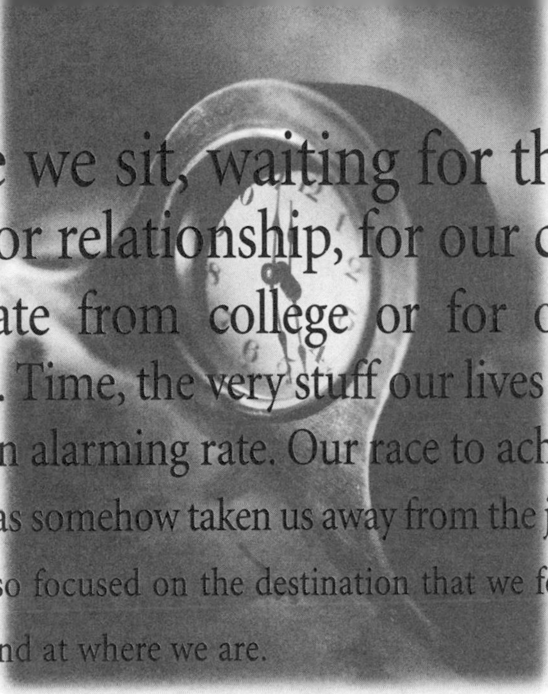

Yet here we sit, waiting for the next big deal or relationship, for our children to graduate from college or for our own retirement. Time, the very stuff our lives are made of, flies at an alarming rate. Our race to achieve these milestones has somehow taken us away from the journey. We have become so focused on the destination that we forget to stop and look around at where we are.

Pleasures, by their very nature, need to be savored. Life is a series of magical moments: a sunset, a long overdue talk with your best friend, a fine cigar at the end of a satisfying meal, being transported to another era by a song on the radio. The cigars and martinis are merely props to be utilized as an entry point to Pleasure, to a better quality relationship with yourself. They are as idiosyncratic and unique as you are. Why not take a look at your life with an eye toward a more pleasurable existence? It is easier than you think, and it is all within your reach.

You don't need to be a multimillionaire to afford a bouquet of freshly cut flowers to grace your nightstand. You don't have to be a movie star to have your shoes meticulously polished. You do not need to be in a relationship to have elegance in your life. But what you do need is imagination, creativity, and a willingness to

Every young actor starting out wants to get a great shot of himself taken by a top photographer. Unfortunately, this wasn't one of them.

try new things. You need to expand your boundaries. And while you're at it, why don't you allow yourself a little wretched excess? It's good for the soul.

Stop for a moment. Unplug from everything and spend a few quiet moments alone with yourself. Think about the richness of the life you have created and be grateful for everything you have. What really makes you happy? When you're having the worst day imaginable, how do you stop the destructive cycle of negative thinking and transport yourself to another place? Is it a special smell that reminds you of your grandmother's kitchen? Is it a song you danced to at your senior prom? Is it a favorite book that touched your heart? Is it the taste of a chocolate truffle? A glass of port? A fine cigar? Or is it watching the clouds change as you take a walk in the park?

One of the hardest things in the world, I find, is to stay in the moment. You can't just live in the future or dwell on the past; you have to shift everything around constantly so that you stay present in those precious moments. Pleasures are what bring you into the moment, and moments are what make up lifetimes.

Be an individual.

Don't try to keep up with everyone else. Be somebody that other people want to emulate. Be you. Be an original. And then the props—the booze, the cigar, the tan, and the Porsche—will merely free you up to be someone unique:

YOURSELF.

Life's

A lazy Sunday

morning in bed

with freshly squ

Little

ezed orange juice,

warm bagels,

and the *New York Times.*

Pleasures

THE BEST OF THE WORST
The Pleasures of Junk Food

Although it is important to eat a balanced, healthy diet most of the time, it is equally important that if you're going to do something that's bad for you, make sure that it is really bad—but in a good way. I'm a firm believer in the 80/20 rule: 80 percent of the time you need to do what's right for your body so you can enjoy the other, slightly decadent, 20 percent of your life. In our society, I think too much emphasis is placed on counting calories and fat grams. The other day I was at the market buying a bag of miniature Milky Way bars (I especially like them frozen), and I was surprised to find a large assortment of fat-free candies. I thought to myself, *A fat-free Three Musketeers? Doesn't that sort of defeat the purpose?* If you want to have a candy bar, then have the real thing. Don't waste the experience on anything less than the best of the worst.

It doesn't take a rocket scientist to know that if you walk into any five-star restaurant, ask for the dessert menu, close your eyes, and point to any item, you can't go wrong. Except, of course, if you order the bread pudding or the fruit compote. But one of the things I have learned is that in the middle of the night, it is very hard to find a decent crème brûlée. Unless you're Elizabeth Taylor, and then the crème brûlée will find you. I remember checking into the Dorchester Hotel in

My take on junk is to avoid it as best you can. But when you slip up, slip up on something like a banana split. If you're going to sin, sin big.

London with Elizabeth late one night. "Do be a dear," she asked me. "Call down to room service and have them send up roast beef with Yorkshire pudding, scones with clotted cream, and a crème brûlée." For a brief moment, I knew instinctively how Eddie Fisher must have felt. But I was hungry, too, so I called downstairs and they informed me that the chef had gone home hours ago, but they would be happy to send up a tray of finger sandwiches. Needless to say, this simply would not do. Elizabeth instructed me to get the chef's home number, call him, and ask him if he wouldn't mind coming in for a few hours to cook dinner for us. I was a little embarrassed, but sure enough, the man got out of bed in the middle of the night, threw on his toque, and raced back to the hotel, where he prepared us a sumptuous repast.

One thing I learned from Elizabeth was, "If you've got it, flaunt it. And when you find some more, flaunt that too."

While we can't all command the great chefs of the world, I'll let you in on a little secret. I think junk food is one of America's greatest national treasures. The French may rave about their pastries, but how can you possibly compare the experience of eating a napoleon, served to you by a sneering waiter, with the pleasures of consuming an entire box of Girl Scout Thin Mints all by yourself? Furthermore, I have never met a Girl Scout who would ever give you any attitude, especially if you bought several boxes of cookies from her. On the other hand, I haven't met any Girl Scouts lately, even though I love a woman in uniform.

If you take the time to look, a lot of good bad food is out there. And it is important to know the difference. I have nothing against them in theory, but most of the fat-free pastries on the market taste like cardboard, and you need a chain saw to cut through them. If I'm going to consume calories and fat grams with reckless abandon and throw my cholesterol count to the wind, I'm going to make sure I find something that is worth the inevitable price I am going to have to pay. If you're an alcoholic who is about to fall off the wagon, the last thing you want someone to offer you is 2 percent beer. And what could be worse than having a fat-free pastry as your last meal? Ask any Death Row inmate, and he'll probably tell you that his last meal is going to be pizza with extra cheese, a cheeseburger, and a hot fudge sundae.

If you're wandering the aisles of your local grocery store late some Saturday night and you see the word Tastycakes, go no further. Peanut Butter Tandy-Takes,

Chocolate Juniors, and Butterscotch Krimpets are true miracles. The packages even have an 800 number so you can have your Tastycakes FedExed to your doorstep. Whereas some people like to combine their Tastycakes with Diet Coke for that combination buzz of sugar and caffeine, I prefer mine with a nice, chilled bottle of very dry champagne—Moet Chandon White Star if you're alone, and Dom Perignon if you're having a guest. If I really need a caffeine fix, a cup of Hamilton's Mocha Java will do the trick. Yes, I'm in the coffee business, too. And if I'm in South Texas and feeling really decadent, I might pick up a bag of pork rinds to add a little salt and fat to the mix, like the Aggies do. If I'm in Indiana, I've been known to drive miles out of my way to find Moon Pies and an RC Cola. Little Debbies have also been an obsession of mine, but it's difficult to ask for a Little Debbie without having the manager of the grocery store try to send you home with one of his nieces.

When it comes to ice cream, the higher the fat content the better. It's true, fat is good. You can't go wrong with Häagen-Dazs or Ben & Jerry's. Carvel Soft Serve with chocolate crunchies sprinkled on top is perfect for a rainy afternoon. "It's It" ice cream bars are a sure winner, although some people prefer Dove Bars. Frankly, I have a hard time with that, because if you've ever seen a melted Dove Bar, you'd realize that nothing that grows on our planet has been used to make it. It reminds me of a chemistry experiment gone wrong.

One of the only reasons I can think of to go to the Midwest is to visit a Dairy Queen (although you'd have thought I've dated enough of them). Dilly Bars are magnificent, as are Buster Bars and Blizzards. And there is nothing quite like a Bing Bar. I don't even want to know how they make the pink filling, but when I'm in Iowa, I buy them by the case. Krispy Kreme doughnuts are worth driving 40 miles out of your way for. Just be sure you buy at least two dozen in case you have to share them.

As far as fast food is concerned, I love a Double Double with everything from In-N-Out Burger.

Pink's hot dogs are a close second to Dodger Dogs. I had a lady friend who was nearly 80 years old and loved to go with me to baseball games. One day I called her up and invited her to go to the ballpark. "I can't go," she said. "I'm on a diet."

I struggled with this concept for a moment before asking her, "Nettie, what does being on a diet have to do with going to a baseball game?"

She replied dryly, "I only go to Dodger games for the hot dogs and the beer and the peanuts. What's the use of driving all the way to Dodger Stadium and sitting through nine innings if I can't eat anything?" I had to admit, she had a point.

Every now and again I sneak into a 7-Eleven for a Hostess Snow Ball and a Dr. Pepper, both of which never make it halfway home. I've even been known to consume an entire Sara Lee frozen cheesecake in one sitting. The first time that happened, I started out eating one tiny little slice at a time until I realized that I had finished half the cake. I was so embarrassed and was always good at covering my tracks, so I decided that the better part of valor was to eat the entire cheesecake. When I'm at the movies, I like Red Hots with my two-ton tub of popcorn. Jujubes and Juicyfruits and Milk Duds always remind me of my childhood. Of course, I wash everything down with Diet Coke.

New York is a treasure trove of great food experiences, junk and otherwise. I, along with many pregnant women, really enjoy garlic pickles on the Lower East Side of Manhattan. I'm not sure when we started thinking bagels were health food, but I prefer Essa onion bagels with a schmear. No fat-free cream cheese for me, despite the fact that I did that commercial. I love a slice of Ray's Original Pizza, or if I'm feeling Sinatraesque, Rockie Lee Chu-Chu Bianco Thin Crust Pizza. Although Zabars gravlax and smoked salmon are certainly not junk food, they are not to be missed. And eating a hot pretzel with mustard while you're walking in midtown Manhattan can take the chill off even the coldest day. But when I'm in the mood for something as cold as Donald Trump's heart and as dry as Bill Gates' wit, I'll take a martini at the 5757 Bar at the Four Seasons Hotel, or a Bloody Mary at the King Cole Bar at the St. Regis, or a Manhattan anywhere. Did you really think I could exist on the pleasures of junk food alone?

Life's

Spending an entire day
indulging yourself with

Little

a good haircut,

a massage,

and an afternoon
of shopping.

Pleasures

Becoming a Domestic God or Goddess

The Pleasures of Self-Sufficiency

Everyone thinks I was born with a silver spoon in my mouth and I never had to polish it myself. On top of that, people think the closest I have ever come to doing housework is hiring a maid. Let me tell you, that is just not the case.

Strange as it may seem, I really enjoy cleaning my house. The book *The Clean Team: Speed Cleaning* by Jeff Campbell (Dell Publishing, 1991) has changed my life. I am positively evangelical about this book. I never thought that I could speak about the bathroom, much less clean one. Until I read this book, a toilet-bowl brush would have just finished me. I thought Formula 409 was the latest cologne from Chanel, Ajax was a mountain I skied down in Aspen, and Hoover was somebody to be avoided at all costs. But armed with a Sony Walkman, rubber gloves, and a gas mask, I have been known to speed clean my own house in 45 minutes, give the maid the day off, and get right back into bed with a box of See's chocolates and a sense of accomplishment akin to that of Martha Stewart. It is, as they say, a damn good thing. I am a fanatic for cleanliness, and one thing I cannot abide in my homes or in my nightclubs is dust. Dusting must be done on a daily basis; like money, it must be continuously moved around. Dust hangs around every day like an annoying old flame. It just keeps coming back despite all best efforts to the contrary.

As a bachelor, one of the biggest romantic disasters is not to have clean sheets. I have told my housekeeper that the sheets are to be changed daily. I'm sure she thinks I must be running a hotel or something. But rest assured, if the wrong color hair winds up on my pillow, I can safely say, "It's the maid's." It's just one less thing to worry about.

My friends constantly laugh at me because I have a penchant for buying household products that I have seen advertised on infomercials. Believe me, when you're alone in a hotel room at two in the morning, clutching a remote control, and trying in vain to sleep on a rock-hard mattress, your Visa card can become a

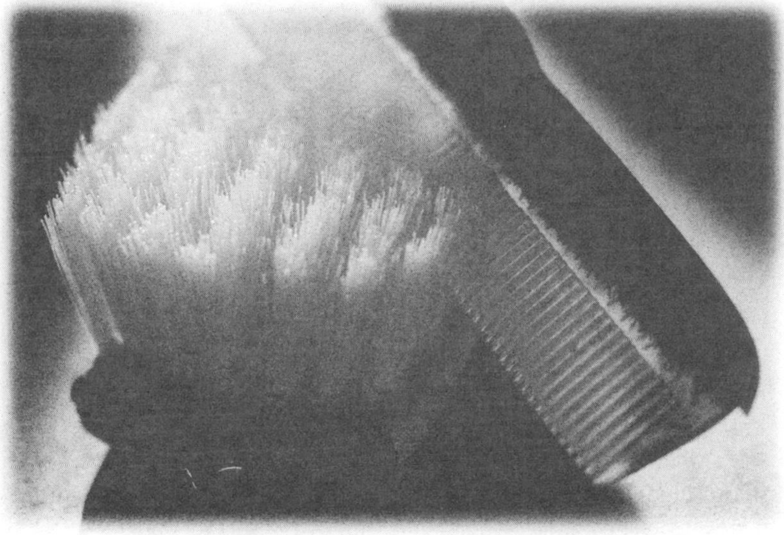

window into an entirely new world. Just be careful if you have a Visa with a high credit limit and you are watching QVC. My newest favorite acquisition is an entire kit designed to make ironing a pleasure—an oxymoron if there ever was one. It includes a Teflon-like cover that fits over your ironing board so that both sides of your clothes are ironed at once. You also get a cover for your iron so that you can iron any fabric without damaging it. The kit also has a cradle for the iron to rest on and a leader for the cord to keep it out of your way while you're ironing. This is so fantastic! It actually irons both sides of your pants with one sweep and makes a perfect crease. You can iron your sheets in 10 minutes flat. And you never have to worry about scorching another shirt. I'm having so much fun doing my own ironing that my housekeeper isn't allowed to iron anymore.

I have also found that rubbing alcohol in a spray bottle works well on windows and countertops. It's much cheaper and smells better than any of the window- or counter-cleaning products I have tried. But if you really want to have a good time, do it my way and substitute vodka. One spray for the windows, two sprays for you.

Cooking is another area of life where self-sufficiency is the order of the day. For a great many years I relied on dining out, which gets boring when your dinner companion is the script you are working on. So I switched to ordering in. I am probably the biggest customer of a Los Angeles–based service called Why Cook? They will deliver just about anything you want from a wide assortment of the finest restaurants in the area, and they will even put it in your own dishes for you!

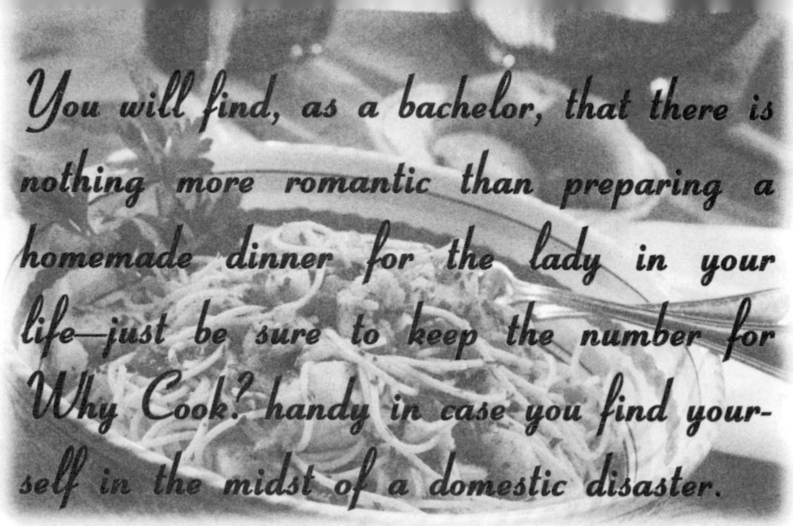

I've been using Why Cook? for so many years, I've started referring to it as Why Eat?

Cooking for one usually creates enough leftovers to provide meals for several weeks. This is where good planning comes in. I have a few simple dishes that I know how to prepare, and I freeze most of the leftovers so that I always have a meal or two on hand. There is nothing better than getting off an airplane after a few weeks away from home where you've existed solely on room service, popping a dish into the microwave, and having a comforting plate of meat loaf in minutes. Start watching the Food Channel on cable to stimulate your imagination. Buy yourself a few cookbooks and find a few signature dishes that you can whip up without too much fuss or trouble.

The satisfaction of being self-sufficient cannot be beat. There's nothing in the world like knowing that you can do it yourself. The contentment of preparing a simple meal, the beauty of a clean home, and the adventure of discovering new and enjoyable ways of cleaning it gives a man a sense of order instead of being ordered. And that is truly one of Life's Little Pleasures.

Life's

Your best friend,
chocolate truffles,

Littl

champagne on ice,
and a Cary Grant
movie on a rainy day.

Pleasures

IT'S THE LITTLE THINGS THAT COUNT

The Pleasures of Relationships

Whether you are a man or a woman, relationships are the easiest thing in the world if you possess the right attitude. For a whole host of reasons, though, it seems to be one area that is universally troubling for both sexes. In the wake of the sexual revolution and the feminist movement, we're all a little confused about our proper roles. Women, it would seem, have traded their superiority for equality. And just about everyone, male and female, is a little bewildered. Thanks to John Gray, we all know that men are from Mars, but women are most definitely from somewhere else altogether. There are also many single women out there who only know how to play by The Rules. Whether you're a woman who loves too much or a man who can't (or won't) commit, romance is fairly simple—especially if you're a man.

Women want to be heard, listened to, and understood. All you have to do is get a woman to talk to you about her feelings and then shut your mouth. If you can do that, you've got her for life, even though one night may be more than enough. I have found that the Socratic questioning technique can get a man through an entire relationship with a woman relatively unscathed. He doesn't have to do anything except ask, "How do you feel about that?" and then clam up. Hum to yourself. Go over the box scores for last night's NBA game in your head if you have to, but keep silent. When she finishes, ask "Really? And then what happened?" When she

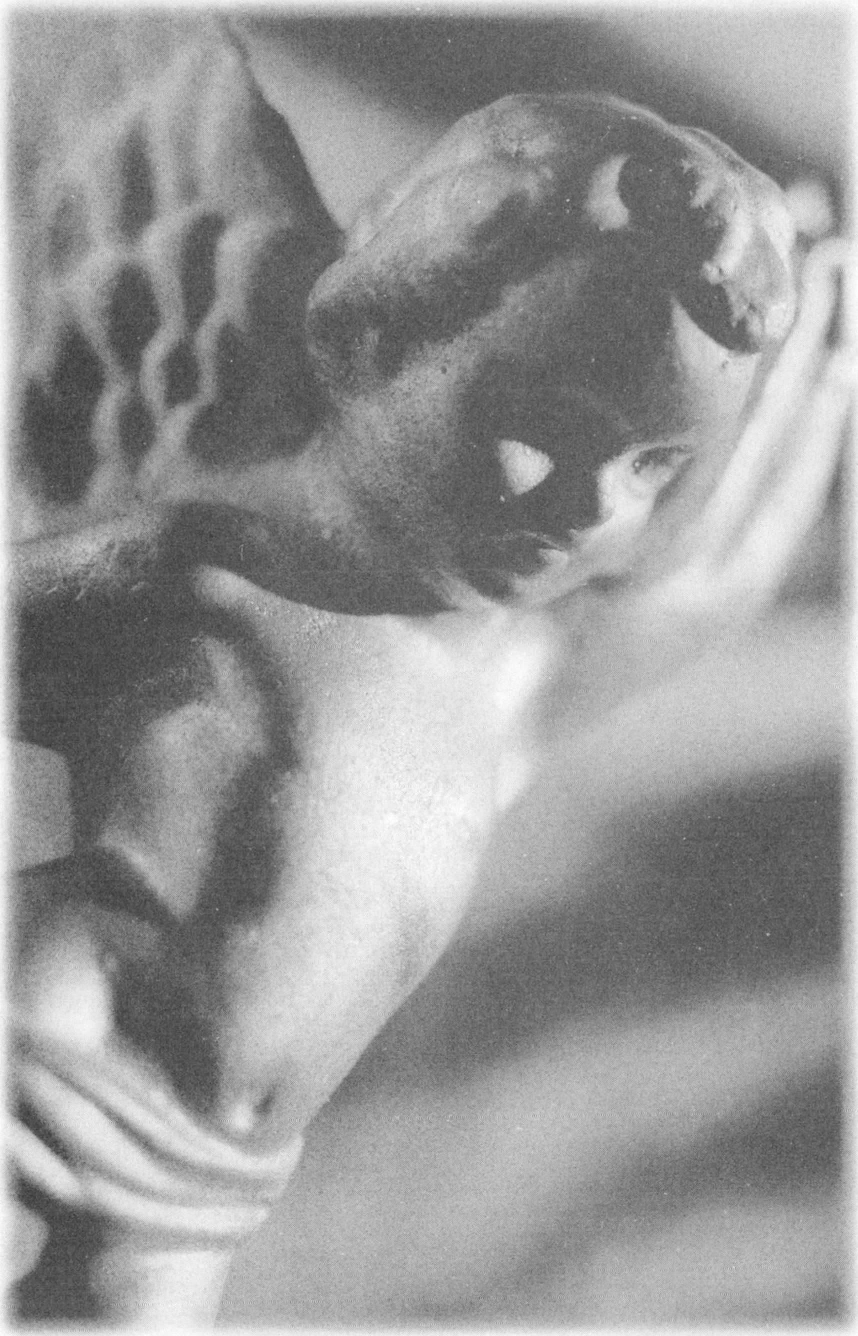

Ever notice how much better a man looks when he has a beautiful woman on his arm? This gorgeous model graced my life all too briefly.

stops ask, "And how did that make you feel?" When she starts to cry (and all women want someone who will let them cry), take out your handkerchief and encourage her to keep on crying. I guarantee that if you follow my suggestions, she will think you are the most sensitive, caring, and adoring man on the planet. Most men make the fatal mistake of trying to fix a woman's problems, and I have learned that women really do not want their problems fixed. When you attempt to fix a woman's problems, you open yourself up to the most indefensible position a man can be in: "You're not listening." Remember, women are smarter than men to begin with. They have already sorted out their own answers over lunch with their girlfriends or at their hairdresser's. What women want most in life is to be heard. And it's your job to listen. Try it sometime. I think you'll be surprised. By the way, I was the one who taught this technique to John Gray…

Whatever you do, when a woman wants to talk, never say to her, "Darling, can I call you back?" To a woman, this translates roughly into "Darling, I couldn't care less about you, and I really need to get to my poker game." Although this may very well be true, it is never wise to let her feel that you have anything else except her needs in mind. Say she calls you at home with a problem just as you're getting ready to leave. Instead of hustling her off the telephone, say, "Tell me about it." That gives you five minutes to shave the right side of your face. Then ask, "And then what happened?" Now shave the left side of your face. You can shower after saying, "That is so unbelievable. Explain it to me one more time. I want to make sure I understand it." When you're finished, continue, "This is really shocking to me. Tell me what else is happening," and then get dressed. So you can take one last look in the mirror and make sure you are pulled together properly, tell her, "Well, you know they really don't understand you, do they?" Just before you head out the door, say, "I wish we had more time to talk, but I know you are so rushed. Why don't you call me back later? You know I'm here for you." Pretty soon you'll be sitting around a table with your best buddies and hearing the four best words any man can hear: "Shut up and deal."

The next essential element is to make a woman feel surrounded by your love. This can be done in simple, inexpensive ways. You don't need to run over to Harry Winston's and pick out some overpriced diamond; women see right through that—with a loop. Call her in the middle of your day and let her know that you are thinking about her. FedEx her a card with a heartfelt note written inside. Have her tennis racket restrung. Wash her car and fill it up with gas. A very wealthy friend of mine swept a woman off her feet by sending her a case of Campbell's Chicken and Stars soup when she was working on a project under a tight deadline.

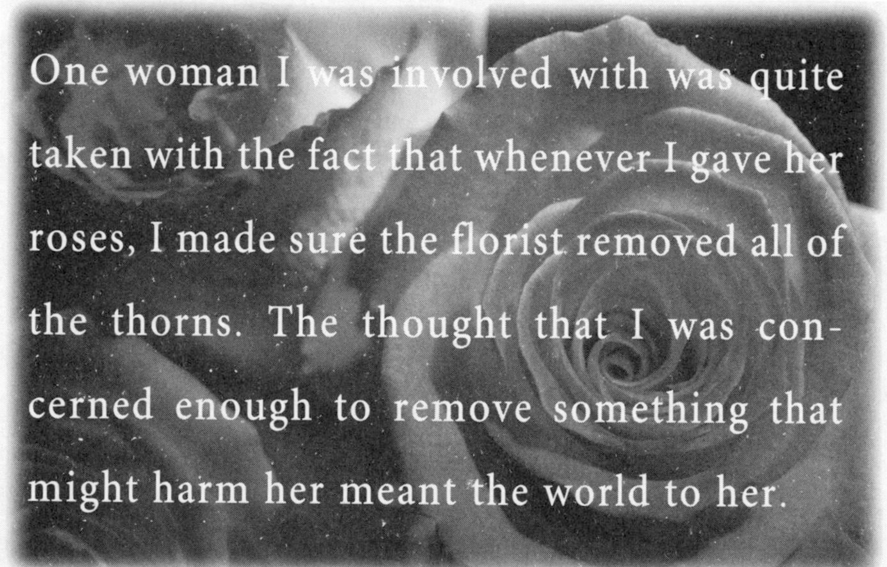

For a woman, the way to a man's heart lies in making yourself indispensable. Surprisingly, it doesn't take much effort on your part. Again, it's the little things that count. Women are natural detectives, and it doesn't take long to size up your man. Is he in the habit of losing his keys, wallet, or papers? As soon as he comes home from work, offer him his favorite drink, put his keys and wallet and briefcase in one spot, and make him a nice dinner. Better yet, after a drink and some pleasant conversation, he will probably feel like taking you out to dinner. Soon he'll be lost without you and he won't know why. A savvy woman I know found out that my favorite childhood candy was Sugar Daddies and surprised me with a box one day. I was incredibly touched. (Unfortunately for me, Sugar Daddies—the live ones—were her favorite, too.) Also, constantly surround your man with friends. Your friends. If your friends become his friends and he leaves you, he will feel as if he is losing his whole life.

What it really comes down to is basic consideration. Treat your partner's needs as though they were your own. Think of the other person as you would think of yourself. It takes a modicum of wit, but when done correctly it can be one of the most pleasurable experiences on Earth.

Nothing is better than making a woman feel like a lady. And nothing will lead faster to an intimate relationship than the presumption that you are not just trying to sleep with her. Make it clear that you are asking her out simply because you enjoy the pleasure of her company. Once you make a woman understand that you find her incredibly attractive and would like to make love with her, but that you will never make a move until she feels she is ready, she will be encouraged to relax and to prepare herself emotionally on her own time. She will think, *Wow, I've really found something here.* And before you know it, she'll be ready. Whenever you take a woman on a trip, never presume you will share a hotel room. Always book two rooms, and at the end of the evening say goodnight to her politely at her door and proceed to your own room. Believe me, by the second night the only thing filling her room will be her luggage. God, why am I giving away all of my secrets? Now it'll take two nights.

It's not what you do; it's how you do it. Make sure the person you are involved with knows that you never forget about him or her. That way, you're never going to be forgotten. If you're in a relationship with someone, you invariably spend some time every day thinking about that person. People love the notion that they're being thought about. Someone who takes the time to think about you is quite special, because most people are basically just thinking about themselves. Constantly keep in mind what brings the other person into your consciousness and how the two of you connect.

Sometimes the best relationships are the ones that are never consummated. One of the absolutely worst things that can happen in life is when a relationship peaks and then we lose the one we love. So often in life we wind up falling in love with people not for what they are, but for what they represent to us. Those who say love is blind are absolutely right. When you look at the one you love, what you are usually seeing are the images and desires you have projected on to that person. It's a fantasy thing, and often reality really doesn't have a lot to do with it.

Wherever I went with Lynda Johnson we were followed by four Secret Service agents, even out on the dance floor. Danger, it appears, was everywhere. It's apparent from the beard I was sporting that I was trying to disguise myself.

Waking up
under
a down comforter

in a country
where nobody
speaks your language.

Pleasures

Set 'em up, Joe

The Pleasures of Divorce

Divorce, although a sad fact of life, can salvage not only a friendship but also, if done correctly, your relationship with yourself. Furthermore, it can be a very interesting process. There is always a choice: Either you can bring in attorneys, which always creates a bad situation, or you can work things out between yourselves. It seems a shame to court a woman, marry her, have a child or two, and then become sworn enemies, but sadly, at a certain point in many marriages, it's time to go down separate roads. It's like the old Charles Aznavour song: You have to leave the table when love is no longer being served. Because our son, Ashley, was involved, it always seemed saner to me to try and remain friends with my ex-wife. You can divorce your spouse, but you can never divorce your children.

Alana and I had been together for more than a decade. You have no idea how strange divorce can be until you try to get a divorce in Hollywood. First there are the Ladies Who Lunch, a fairly acrimonious group whose members are being supported in style by a retinue of former husbands. Nothing angers this group more than a happy marriage, because in a way it nullifies their own bitter divorces. They are rooting for your marriage to fail, and if they enter the picture, you're doomed.

Now, men's lunches are totally different. You can have a heart-to-heart talk with a man and he won't ever hold it against you. After a few Crown Royals, a man will

Love is better the second time around. Well…maybe yes, maybe no. But at least my talk show with my ex-wife Alana proved we could still be friends.

Here's a picture of Alana and me when we ran away to Las Vegas to get married. We didn't have time to round up a best man, so we brought along our best dog, Georgie.

usually forget everything you have told him anyway—that is, of course, assuming that he was listening to you in the first place.

Then come the therapists, psychics, and astrologers. Alana and I once went to a therapist who was so wacky, he emptied a bag of M&M's onto the table at the beginning of our session. As we talked about the disintegration of our union, he proceeded to arrange the M&M's in rows according to color, and began to eat one from each row every minute. When he finished the M&M's, the session was over. It was sort of like the blind leading the deaf.

I have to admit I've had my moments as well. My low period came when I went to one of the leading therapists who specialized in finding your inner child. There I was, saying to a doll on my lap, "What does little Georgie want today?" when the therapist asked if she could cut our session short because she had a hair appointment. My next strategy for saving my marriage was to hire a nutritionist. Fortunately, everyone in Hollywood at the time was suffering from low blood sugar or high blood sugar, attention deficit disorder, and countless other designer ailments including Epstein-Barr. The nutritionist did nothing to help our marriage, but the rush from the niacin he prescribed was well worth the cost of admission.

Over martinis and cigars the other night, an acquaintance of mine from San Antonio informed me that he has been separated for two years from his wife of 23 years and that they were now seeing their third therapist together. Clearly, he wanted to make sure they tried every avenue available to them before The Inevitable. The problem, you ask? Well, it seems she was the one who wanted to leave him, which is never easy for a man's ego. Even though he had fallen out of love with her long ago, a divorce was not a loss that he could afford, emotionally or financially. For this poor, unfortunate soul, she had beaten him to the punch.

Not long after their youngest child was enrolled in college and their dog had run away, she got a job, an apartment of her own, and a (hopefully) wealthy boyfriend in another city, and she moved out. He admitted that if he had been the one to leave her, the marriage would have been over 18 months ago.

After he calculated the possible financial ramifications of a divorce, he wondered if leading a life of not-so-quiet desperation might be the saner economic move. He tried without much success to win her back, then auditioned every therapist in San Antonio until he found the one that would tell him what he wanted to hear: that he was young, virile, and in demand (despite being broke), and that his wife had deep-seated emotional problems that she needed to deal with on her own. It would be better if he let her go, even though the divorce was her idea to begin with. He emerged from this therapy session with his ego intact and unscathed. He felt noble again, and promptly called his lawyer.

In Hollywood, if you're a man of any means who is as smart as he is manipulative, you try to "buy" your therapist. As a rule of thumb, the therapist usually goes to the highest bidder. There are exceptions, but generally if a therapist tells you something vague like "I can't tell you that it's going to work out, but whatever happens it's going to be the best thing for you," at that point you should buy your therapist. Not with cash, but by promising to refer all your friends' troubled relationships and divorces to him or her, and if all else fails, a publishing deal for his or her latest psychotherapy technique.

When we realized that our divorce was inevitable, I went to Alana, who is a very bright woman, and said, "Listen. Having loved you, I now stoop to being your friend because we have a son together. Let me advise you as a friend would. This plate, which represents everything that we have together—any way you figure it, one half of it is yours and one half of it is mine. The perfect deal in life is to cut the plate in half and let you choose which half you want. But at the end of the day, you will still get only half of the plate. Now the lawyers will tell you what they think should happen, but while they are doing that, they're going to get a section of the plate to pay for their summer home, and I'd much rather have it go to you."

I then offered her, as an incentive, the cash equivalent of the cost of fighting a difficult court battle, if she would sit down and negotiate the settlement with me

Alana and I will always be joined by our mutual concern for our son, Ashley. To me it's the most pleasant of bonds. Alana is my best friend. I could go to her with any problem and she would offer me her best wishes.

without involving any lawyers. She agreed, and we examined our assets: cash, stock, real estate, cars, and whatever was left of the wreckage of my career. We figured out 17 different scenarios, which were all of equal value financially. Alana was to choose the one that made her feel the most protected. Contrary to the big-ticket divorces that make the headlines, there are reasonable women out there who simply need enough money to live in the same manner they would if you were still married: a roof over their head, money to pay the bills, and a car they wouldn't be embarrassed to valet park. We were lucky; Alana did not use our divorce as a weapon to try and bludgeon me. We never had a single argument over money. We are still the best of friends, proof positive that sometimes it takes a divorce to salvage a friendship. We even did a talk show together. The one intangible in our divorce: To sweeten the deal I insisted that she get custody of Hollywood. A tragedy.

Nothing is worse than the insecurity you feel after a divorce. It's different for each sex. A man doesn't start to feel a sense of loss until after the ink is dry on the divorce papers, and not a moment before. This is because during the process he has managed to convince himself that this is just another negotiation. Soon he will be free, his youth regained. Just one more microweave, a teeth bleaching, a minituck, and he's ready to rumba. Divorce is much easier for a woman because in her own mind, she was gone long before she left you. Not unlike my friend in San Antonio, men spend the entire separation period in denial; they can't believe it's really over. Take it from me: Once a woman leaves you, it's really over. No amount of pleading or therapy or romantic weekend getaways will change her mind. She's already joined the gym, found a new hairdresser, and graduated from Outward Bound. A man, in the meantime, is swilling Jack Daniel's, listening endlessly to Frank Sinatra crooning "One for My Baby," and trying to convince his friends that his ex-wife really wants a reconciliation.

I was such a lunatic after my divorce that I used to drive around my old neighborhood in my very inconspicuous lemon meringue–colored Rolls-Royce. It got so bad that, one evening, when I stopped in front of Alana's house, she opened her window and asked me what I was doing there, and I blithely answered, "Shopping for real estate." The fact that it was two in the morning did not help my case any.

It's hell to be a guy, because three drinks on the wrong night and you'd better believe you'll be dialing your ex-wife's number. Men, do yourselves a favor. Don't leave a message. And pray she doesn't have Caller ID.

Life's

Creating a daily set of rituals for yourself

Little

that makes your life
more meaningful.

Pleasures

SEEKING SERENITY WITHIN

The Pleasures of the Soul

I don't care who you are or how powerful, wealthy, rich, successful, talented, charming, or smart you are. Sooner or later, in even the most charmed life, something bad is going to happen. I'm a firm believer that it's not what happens in your life, but how you react to it that determines what kind of person you are. It's easy to be a holy man on the side of a mountain, but it's hard as hell to be one in Beverly Hills. How you handle life's inevitable ups and downs is a true test of character. One way or another, we're all going to be brought to our knees, and when you're at that point, there's only one way to look—and that's up.

We all take life—and time—for granted. We assume that we and our loved ones have endless vistas of bad decisions ahead of us and plenty of time to waste. Money and fame and power can come and go. I should know. The most important commodity is time, so don't allow yourself to waste it. If you do, it could very well be the biggest mistake you can make, because Father Time is the meanest man in town. But life can change in an instant. Turn on CNN some night if you doubt me. It's important to believe in something that is bigger than your ego, your bank account, or your toys. The two most important lessons I have learned in my life are: Never cry over anything that doesn't love you back, and any problem that can be solved with money really isn't a problem to begin with.

Although religion these days has become quite chic, there's nothing I hate worse

than "cocktail party spirituality." I know you're probably thinking that the only thing I have ever worshiped in my life is the sun. Not true. I have also worshipped girls in the sun. You may think I've prayed at a baccarat table for a 9. Well, I've also prayed for my date at a baccarat table to get a 9, and I've dated some 10s. See? I'm not as shallow as you might think. I came from a unique family. My grandfather was a small-town doctor, and my grandmother was a Christian Science practitioner. Either way they were covered. They were quite a couple. I remember my grandfather saying to me that when it came to healing people, he really had never done much on his own medically; if anything, medicine may have gotten in the way of people's healing.

Even with my family history, spirituality came to me, as it does for most people, when I was at my wit's end and had no choice but to surrender to any power, let alone a higher one. My faith has upheld me when everything seemed to be working against me. It's helped me to overcome adversity and transform it to my advantage.

It's nice to have all those high-priced toys, but most people try to fill up the empty spaces in their souls with them. Your leased Montreal blue BMW Z3 makes you feel great until you realize that her new boyfriend has a sapphire blue Jaguar XK8. Worse yet, he paid cash. Your satellite dish is not as small as your neighbor's. Armani's spring line always follows the fall, and so on. What are you going to rely on to make you feel good to be in your own skin? No relationship, no job, no clothes, no amount of money will genuinely help. All that stuff comes and goes.

you

So, are you going to tap into that pool of stillness that resides within, from which originates everything that animates you? Buddha, Christ, Lao-tse, and Shakespeare all said basically the same thing: It's really all about you. When are you going to spend a few moments being grateful for everything you do have, instead of whining about everything you don't? When are you going to remember that a prayer is not some sort of wish list that you hand over to God the way you fill out an order form from the J. Crew catalog? Prayer is about having the grace to transcend your circumstances, not asking for a ticket out of them. You really discover who you are when your back is up against the wall. That's when you find out if you have been learning the lessons you are supposed to learn.

Hollywood is a state of mind. One of the secrets of the game is that it's all about perception—yours as well us that of the people who surround you. For me, reality grew out of that notion. I spent many years collecting bits of other people's personalities and weaving them into George Hamilton before I stopped and tried to figure out who George Hamilton really was. One of the keys to my longevity is that I really have never taken myself too seriously. I also have always had incredible faith and a strong spiritual background. I believe in gratitude. I believe in living in the moment and trying to remain positive.

Life is totally an adventure for me. It's tragic that we give credence to the notion that we need certain things in place in our lives in order to be truly happy and that we have an endless amount of time to figure our lives out. My belief is that the adventure lies in letting go and just enjoying the ride. Sure, it's wonderful to have a map and a heading, but you'd better allow for some drift because there's going to be some. Sometimes I like to tear up the map completely. I like getting lost because I enjoy the challenge of finding my way back. I have absolutely no fear about life in the least. I think the longer you live and the more you experience in your life, the easier you are on yourself. I don't berate myself as much as I used to. I just learn the lesson and move on. It's one of the few gifts of growing older. Although there have been many times when I have been broke, I have never been poor. Poor is a state of mind, a cloud that you can't get out from under. Being broke is a temporary front that is just passing through.

A wise man once said that the people who never make mistakes are the people who never do anything in life. I know a lot of men who haven't lived one third of the life I have lived. The bad things that have happened to me I believe have happened for a reason. I'm responsible for a good part of it. There are lessons to be learned and I am open to them. And if I had my life to live over again, I wouldn't change a thing. (Except for the Nehru jacket that I wore on *The Ed Sullivan Show.* There was absolutely no reason for that.)

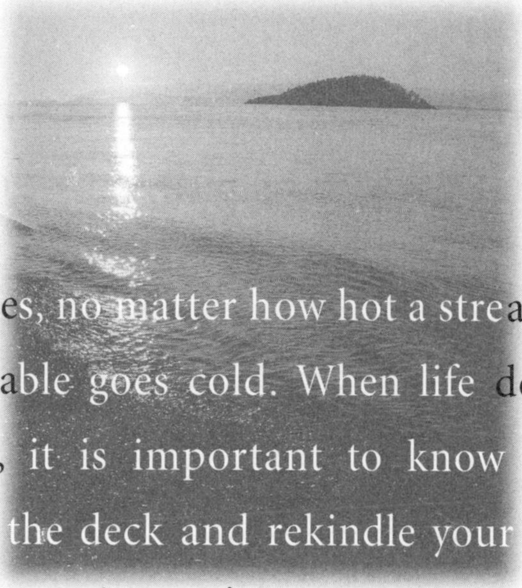

Sometimes, no matter how hot a streak you're on, the table goes cold. When life deals you adversity, it is important to know how to reshuffle the deck and rekindle your passion for life. Sometimes it's as simple as listing all the things you are truly grateful for. Or taking a long, hot bubble bath. Or enjoying a milk shake. Or watching a sunset. Or playing Monopoly with your children. The reason why Pleasure is such an important concept is that it can become another tool in your arsenal for dealing with life's inevitable letdowns.

You have to possess the grace not to take yourself too seriously. You came into this world alone and you're going to go out of this world alone, and everything you do in between should be a helluva lot of fun.

After all, you're born naked, you're probably going to die naked, and with any luck, some of the best days of your life will be spent naked. And while it's nice to acquire material things, I've never seen a U-Haul following a hearse. The fact of the matter is, life goes by in an instant. Many people waste time sitting on the sidelines waiting to get picked for the team instead of running out on the field and creating their own game.

One of the most appealing attributes any human being can possess is a passion and a zest for life. It is positively contagious. I have a lady friend who is attractive but not a great beauty, yet she always seems to be surrounded by the most incredible men. After getting to know her better, I learned her secret: She's happy to be alive, and her joyfulness and effervescence captivate everyone she comes into contact with. She's as excited about a patty melt at the corner coffee shop as she is thrilled to be dining out at '21'. Her playful spirit and sense of adventure makes everyone in her presence feel like they have been let in on one of life's great secrets.

Passion for life is something that is truly lacking in even the most successful people. They keep wanting the external events of their lives—their successes, relationships, toys, money—to imbue their lives with meaning. And we all know that consuming your way into a fulfilling life is like trying to blow up a balloon that has a hole in it. If you are relying on circumstances and people outside of you to create a sense of fulfillment, you are doomed to an existence in which too much is never enough.

Nothing is more interesting than talking to someone who is passionate about her or his work. In a perfect world, your vocation should be your avocation. You should strive to do work that you enjoy, that feeds your soul in some way. Your career shouldn't be just about the paycheck or the promotion, it should be something that you feel excited about. I really enjoy acting, and I have a tremendous passion for it. When you have a passion for your work, you really have no fatigue. I had an agent very early on in my career who told me that if being an actor ever becomes work, I should get out of the business. I still don't understand why people get paid to be an actor; it's the easiest job in the world, and when you have a good script and a great director, it's absolute magic. Working in a collaborative medium such as film is pure bliss for me. Whereas I'm incredibly reverent to the process of moviemaking, I'm incredibly irreverent to myself within the process.

There are times in your life when you need to stop thinking about yourself for a while and start thinking about helping others. It's one of the greatest pleasures around.

One area that is constantly overlooked is spending time in service to good causes. You don't need to be a wealthy philanthropist to be a contributor. There are many opportunities to volunteer within your very own community. One of the reasons I enjoy doing charity work is because, quite frankly, it makes me feel good. It feels so good that it's almost one of the most selfish things a person can do. This is going to sound corny, but everything you give, you get back a hundredfold, minus agents' fees and taxes. Everyone has some unique skill and talent, and there will always be a child who needs a mentor, an elderly woman in a nursing home who would like to have someone listen to her stories, or a shut-in who would enjoy being read to. Whenever you are feeling down, and those times do come in life, take yourself out and do something nice for someone else. You'll be doing something for yourself as well. Not only will you learn things about yourself, but you'll uncover qualities you never knew you had.

Spirituality is one of the greatest journeys you can take. Go to church or synagogue. Take a walk along the beach or in the mountains. Go out into a field and watch the plants grow. Unplug the telephone and spend 20 minutes in silence. Think about all the things you have to be grateful for. Meditate.

Then go have a martini.

Life's

Buying your first custom

Little

made monogrammed shirt.

Pleasures

SMOKE GETS IN YOUR EYES...

But Not If You Light It Properly

The Pleasures of Cigars

I'm absolutely thrilled by the cigar renaissance. It is wonderful to walk into a bar nowadays (everywhere, that is, except California, where they will shoot you if you light up anything) and see people bonding over a good cigar. People are coming together and speaking to one another again. You see, it takes a certain time commitment to smoke a cigar—anywhere between 45 minutes to an hour and a half, depending on the size. The time spent between lighting up and that last savory puff is usually best spent sharing a good conversation. A glass of port, a single malt scotch, or a cup of well-brewed coffee only enhances the cigar experience.

People enjoy cigars for myriad reasons that are as unique as their personalities. For instance, although I usually enjoy a cigar at the end of a social evening, occasionally I enjoy smoking when I am alone. Camaraderie is one thing, but sometimes I like to sit down with a good book or some nice music on the stereo and experience a cigar all by myself. When I smoke a cigar, I disengage. My thoughts grow very quiet. A cigar becomes a mini-vacation that allows me time to ponder. I think people first started smoking cigars because they thought it was some sort of status symbol. To me, a cigar is all about contemplation. When I smoke, the

Your jokes grow stale, your hair recedes, the woman of your dreams leaves you for a man half your age…but a good cigar never fails you. Anything that loyal I have to own. That's why I created my own cigar company.

ephemeral becomes tangible. The drink and the cigar are not necessarily long lasting, but they extend the moment for me. They are the props that crystallize the experience. And I think that is what people are looking for. We all live our lives in a series of moments, and when I take the time to commune with myself, I can savor those moments.

Mostly, however, I enjoy the cigar as an adjunct to good conversation. It's one of the oldest bonding rituals that I know of. A cigar can be used to commemorate a special event: a wedding, the birth of your first grandchild, the fact that it is Tuesday afternoon. Oddly enough, a cigar can create a level playing field between men and women. As an enlightened male chauvinist, I have to tell you that there is nothing sexier than a woman who really knows how to smoke a cigar. And if she can smoke a cigar and talk intelligently about sports at the same time, she has captured my absolute attention. Whereas many women make a point of asking their men to take their cigars outside, I appreciate a woman who not only enjoys but also encourages cigar smoking in her home. Cigar smoking is one pleasure a woman can share with the man in her life. I even know a group of women who have made cigars a part of their weekly girls-only poker game.

Smoking a cigar should be an event. Enjoying the ritual and ceremony involved, as well as celebrating the moment, is what cigar smoking is all about. Done correctly, cigar smoking bespeaks a certain level of elegance and refinement. Done incorrectly, it can make you look like an outtake from a Marx Brothers movie featuring your weird uncle Murray and those Swisher Sweets that your aunt Gussie wouldn't let him smoke in the house.

Some men know exactly what brand of cigar they like; these are usually the same men who can spend $10,000 over the course of a weekend in ones, fives, and tens at the local strip club. I have always felt that part of the pleasure of cigar smoking lies in experimenting and trying new and different things. Not unlike learning about fine wine, cigar smoking is about educating your palate. Many good guidebooks can help you through the learning curve. *Cigar Aficionado* magazine has a rating system in each issue that describes the particular characteristics of a certain type of cigar. Your choice often depends on whether you are having your cigar before dinner, after dinner, or with a drink. It also depends on the time of day. Surprisingly, your size and temperament must also be taken into account. What some people fail to realize is how much a cigar eventually takes on the personality of the person who smokes it. If a person is nervous and puffs on the cigar a lot, the cigar will heat up and become more acidic.

Smoking a cigar is really based on what you're doing and what you like, and on how much time you want to spend smoking. A truly fine cigar can last at least five minutes without being puffed on at all. The last thing you want to do is to have to relight. To me, there is an art to keeping a conversation going, and smoking should be kind of a natural extension of that conversation. I don't think a cigar should ever remain in the mouth for long periods of time, and you should never speak with a cigar in your mouth either. It's tacky.

There are so many different approaches to cutting a cigar: piercing, the V-cut, the guillotine or double guillotine. It's all a matter of taste, but the biggest mistake that people make is cutting too deeply. This causes the cigar to eventually unravel in your mouth, and you will end up looking like Ernie Kovacs. The last one-sixteenth of the cap holds the structure of the cigar together, so you must make sure to get a good, clean cut.

Lighting a cigar is usually done too fast because the smoker is nervous. Take your time and light the cigar carefully. And never light a cigar for anybody else. If you

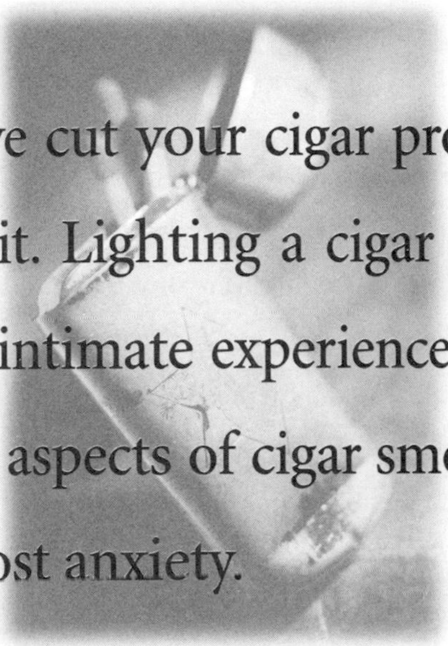

Once you have cut your cigar properly, it is now time to light it. Lighting a cigar is an incredibly personal and intimate experience. Unfortunately, it's one of the aspects of cigar smoking that cause people the most anxiety.

do, he or she might feel obligated to rush, and consequently their cigar won't light properly and will look foolish. A gentleman should light his own, then hand his lighter to his companion so that each can go about it at his or her own speed. Candles are very romantic, but they are not good for lighting a cigar. Lighter fluid definitely creates the smell of gas. Butane has a cleaner smell. A plain wooden match is a good way to go, once you let the sulfur burn off. Usually it takes at least four or five minutes to dispel the charcoal-burned taste, but once you're past that point, you're in for the best hour of your day, if not your week.

Everyone has his or her own style of smoking a cigar, but a good rule of thumb is to remember that your pinkie should never, ever be up in the air—it makes you look like a sharpie or a blackjack dealer. The cigar should never leave your hand, except when you place it in an ashtray. Chewing on the head of a cigar is a sure sign of either a rank amateur or a lawyer and shows incredibly bad form. It also damages the cigar and renders it almost impossible to smoke. While smoking, it is important to remember never to inhale; simply pretend you're Bill Clinton. Keep the tip up at all times, and make sure the ash does not fall on your clothing. On a good cigar, the ash should burn off white in color and should hold for at least one inch before falling off. Generally speaking, the paler the ash, the finer the cigar. Never flick a cigar ash in the same manner you would flick a cigarette. The ash is essential because it helps keep the temperature of the smoke down. After you gently tip your ash into the ashtray, allow the cigar a few moments to cool down before taking your next puff.

One should smoke a cigar until it is no longer pleasing to the palate, which is usually about two-thirds of the way down. Even the most expensive cigar will eventually taste like a nickel stogie if you smoke it too long. If you've gotten all the way down to the band, stop. It's considered incredibly bad form and could very well cause the band to catch fire. Unless you're Jim Carrey, don't try this at home. Simply place the cigar in an ashtray and allow it to die a natural death. Stubbing it out is a sure sign of a rube.

If you practice cigar smoking enough, people will think you are smooth, elegant, stylish, and in control. When in doubt, imagine you're me. That's more difficult than you think; after all, it's taken me almost 59 years to figure out who I am.

Life's

A bubbling hot Jacuzzi

on a star-fillec

Littl

evening in Aspen,

with bottles of
Dom Perignon icing
down in the snowbanks.

Pleasures

TO HAVE AND TO HAVE NOT

The Pleasures of Money, Power, and Fame

As an actor, I learned early on that almost everyone I met wanted to be a movie star—or thought they looked as good as one. President Lyndon Johnson once turned to me and asked, "When they make a movie of my life story, who do you think would play me best, John Wayne or Gregory Peck?" I said, "Let me think about that for a minute and get back to you."

Although many actors will tell you how horrible it is to be famous, I have found fame to be the great one-upmanship of life. When I was working with the devoted Method actor, George Peppard (a talented man despite that series *The A-Team*), he tried to convince me that I needed to learn to become a Method actor, because that was the only way to go. One day, a young boy came up to us with his autograph book. He looked at Peppard and asked, "Excuse me, sir, are you a movie star?"

George gave the child a withering look and said, "No, I'm not a movie star, I'm an actor." The child shrugged, looked at me and asked, "Are you an actor?"

I replied, "No, I'm not an actor, I'm a movie star," and promptly signed his book.

That day I drew a line that changed my whole career. From that moment on, I took my work seriously, but I never took myself seriously.

I know what President Lyndon Johnson was thinking behind his wide Texan smile. "If this Hollywood pretty boy thinks he's worming his way into the White House by marrying my daughter, he has another thing coming. I'll have the SOB drafted and sent to Vietnam."

Here we are as the royal family: my mother, my brothers Bill and David, and me.

When I was growing up, my family never had any real money of our own, yet we surrounded ourselves with millionaires and people who had everything. I looked around and decided pretty quickly that these people really weren't happy. I knew fairly early in the game that money wasn't everything—you've got to include the interest, too. But I was like a greyhound racing behind a mechanical rabbit. Whatever "it" was, it was just out of reach. I wanted to prove myself, and that gave me the drive to go further and do more and be like them. Somehow, in the process, I managed to surpass their own happiness. God bless the child that got his own.

I attended Hackley, an exclusive prep school in New York. Very "old money"—and we had *new* money, *so* new we were still waiting for it. I was surrounded by guys who were dressed in the latest styles. I went to thrift shops. Haunted them, actually. I would pore over the racks and find clothes that millionaires wore in the 1920s. I'd end up buying jackets for five dollars with no lining in them, but they were beautifully tailored and fitted. I'd show up at some girl's coming-out party and be the best-dressed guy there. When I opened up my jacket, there would be holes in the lining, and I'd explain, "My father's or my grandfather's." And they'd all say, "How chic!" I lived in two jackets. I learned early on that it was the little things in life that made all the difference.

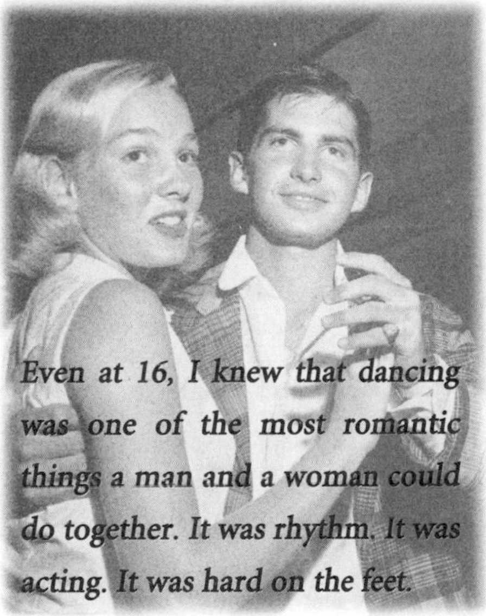

Even at 16, I knew that dancing was one of the most romantic things a man and a woman could do together. It was rhythm. It was acting. It was hard on the feet.

I remember sitting in the El Morocco nightclub one evening when I was 18 years old. Onassis at one table and Vanderbilt at another. They were both looking at Errol Flynn, who was entering the room. I noticed the difference in their styles. One was effusive and grand, the other staid and proper. I saw, sitting 12 feet apart, the difference between new money and old money and I thought to myself, *Now which one am I, since I haven't got* any *money*? So I chose the one path that would make them both jealous. I chose to become a movie star.

We were a close family. It would appear from this photo that we held hands wherever we went. Here we are in Palm Beach showing off the latest sportswear.

Oddly enough, I would have been happy to have become a doctor. For as long as I can remember, my mother and older brother wanted to be movie stars. My mother was the daughter of a doctor and the matriarch of a small town. They were well-off, but by no means rich. My mother was sent to a boarding school in New York, and from that moment on she had her eye on glamour. After she divorced my father, she returned to her hometown in Arkansas with my older brother and myself. Then both of her parents died within a month of each other, and this string of events shattered her "princess" image. She then entrusted her dreams to the care of my older brother, and in 1947 we moved to Hollywood so they could become actors.

As a child, I saw Hollywood in its heyday and my mother truly was the belle of the ball. I saw movie stars up close, and I had the sense that although my mother and brother were never going to become stars, it would eventually become my destiny to fulfill the dream for them. Even though we had no money, we always managed to live in a lavish manner. When I needed to go to MGM to negotiate my first contract, I bought an old Rolls-Royce that had been in an accident and didn't have a back end. I took it to a body shop that was run by an out-of-work actor and promised him that if he fixed my car for free, I would get him a role in a movie. He did the whole back end of the car in Bondo for me. I hired the next-door neighbor's gardener to pose as my chauffeur and we drove to MGM in a car that was bigger and grander than anything Gloria Swanson had ever been driven in. In the midst of my negotiations with the studio heads, they offered to get me a car through the studio's credit union. I told them I already had a car, but it was borrowed from my mother and I really wanted something a little more contemporary. They were about to offer me a Chrysler when they looked out the window and saw my "chauffeur" standing on the running board of the Rolls-Royce. They then doubled the salary offer that was on the table. With that money I bought myself a Bentley. I had succeeded in creating the perception of great wealth, and that has been the story of my entire life and career. I have lived well all of my life, and people don't offer me less money because of this perception, they offer me more.

From my very first day in the movies, I sent checks home to my family. I had to work to support my mother and my brothers, and sometimes that forced me to make compromises. I bought a 39-room mansion that had once belonged to Douglas Fairbanks because my brother told me that is what movie stars did. I had just enough money for the down payment, but not enough to support a lavish lifestyle. It was a little annoying to come home from working on a picture only to have my brother Bill show me some expensive antique chair he bought that we simply could not live without, and I'd have to leave the next day to do a play so we could pay for it. But it was all part of the amusing madness my family created. While Warren Beatty was getting the film roles I wanted, I was away doing summer stock or being billed above the roast beef at some obscure dinner theater. I'd come back to Hollywood with a deep tan, and people would ask me where I had been. I'd answer, "The Riviera" or "Palm Beach on vacation." I lived out my family's fantasies because it was what they wanted. They had the parties and whatnot, and my career provided them with social cachet. Stardom became my way of standing out and of earning love from my family.

Having always rubbed shoulders with millionaires, I have found them to be a fairly discontented lot. Everybody thinks that having money can guarantee you a pleasurable life. Well, it's not about money. Being born into money can often be the worst thing in the world that can happen to you. It can destroy your desire to be someone, and it can make you look at your life in terms of everything you have to lose rather than everything you have to gain. Most people, when they are halfway up a mountain, find that their desire for gain is exactly equal to their fear of losing what they've got. So they stand there, completely stifled and paralyzed with fear. Once they've earned their money, they always worry that someone will steal it, or worse, that their idiot children will waste it.

Thank you very much. Thank you. Thank you. Elvis has left the building and he's posing for pictures with Col. Tom Parker, Lynda Johnson, and yours truly.

I do believe there comes a point where too much money will destroy you. It always surprises me that some of the wealthiest people I know think I have the best life imaginable. I fill up my day in the sun, worrying about the tailor or whether to have another glass of wine with lunch, while they are worried about which corporation they are going to take over next. I've always wanted to be them, and it turns out they have always wanted to be me. And as I build my tiny lifestyle empire, I realize they were right. It's so much easier to be rich and famous and a movie star than to create and run an empire.

I once asked the head of a country which he would rather have: fame, money, or power. He took a gun out of a drawer, placed six bullets in the chamber, put it on the table and pointed to it. "You see that gun?" he said. "If I were to fire one of those bullets, I'm less powerful. It's the threat that makes you powerful, and power will bring you all the rest—money and fame. Be powerful first, and then everyone will throw money and fame at you."

Well, I have never been powerful, but I've certainly been surrounded by a lot of

A proud moment and a big day—Ashley and I at the inauguration of President George Bush. I remember thinking that presidents come and go, but actors—well...I guess they come and go too.

powerful people, and I have realized they are enslaved by that rush of power. I've never really had that feeling; it's not in my nature. But I have to admit that I've always sort of admired it and enjoyed being around it.

While I've often wondered if power is better to have than fame or money, there is always a moment where a powerful and wealthy man wants to be famous. I remember going to President George Bush's inauguration. I had been one of the few actors who supported him early in his campaign. My son, Ashley, and I arrived in Washington and were treated like royalty. We went to every party, had breakfast with Sununu, and spent the morning with the president. Walking right in front of us at the inauguration was none other than Donald Trump. Donald was waving at the crowd as though he was the one who had just been elected president. Ashley asked me, "Who is that man? Nobody seems to know or care who he is. Is he a politician?" I said no.

"Is he an actor?"

"No."

"Well, then, who is he?"

I said, "He's The Donald."

"Ronald McDonald?" Ash asked.

"No," I said, "but something like that."

Donald Trump was so taken with his own celebrity that he went all the way down to the first row only to find there were no seats for him. At that point, he started a slow retreat back up the aisle and smiled at me as he passed us. After he went by I said, "Ash, follow me."

As we went down the aisle Ashley was muttering, "Oh, Dad. No. Please. This is so embarrassing." When we got to the front row, I saw two empty seats next to a Marine captain who was standing at attention. I said, "Captain, I'm George Hamilton and this is my son and we're supposed to have two seats in the front row."

He said, "Yes sir, right here, sir," and we were seated immediately. Then the Marine added, "I loved you in *Evel Knievel*."

It illustrated brilliantly to my son the difference between Donald Trump and myself: He's powerful, but I'm famous. And it also goes to prove my old military school training: Don't ever ask. Expect and command, and a Marine will always come through for you. Semper Fi.

Life's

A hot-air balloon ride
at sunrise

Little

and toasting
the morning with a glass
of fine champagne.

Pleasures

LIQUOR, LADIES, AND LUCK

The Pleasures of Doing It My Way

For Frank Sinatra and the rest of the Rat Pack, Pleasure was all about booze, broads, and bets. But if we're doing this My Way, Pleasure is about liquor, ladies, and luck—separately or taken in combination (unless, of course, you are prone to excess).

I enjoy alcohol. I think it's really one of the greatest mood alterers we have. It's based on sugar, and it goes right to your stomach. If you think about it that way, however, there's absolutely no romance in it at all. I'm enchanted by the idea that something is very old and aged. Something, that is, besides myself. Clearly, somebody got it right. Probably it was that friar who invented champagne. The whole secret of alcohol is in the lack of abuse of it. If you respect it, it is something you can enjoy your whole life. If you don't respect it, you might as well drink the cheapest stuff there is. Let's face it, after the third drink it doesn't matter if you give a guy the most expensive scotch or the cheapest rotgut. Alcohol is best in moderation, as part of meal taking or socializing. It is truly something that you can have a relationship with. People are always looking for a prop that provides an entry point to their inner selves. Alcohol is definitely one of them, but only when used in a nonabusive way. For me, a double martini has an almost psychotropic effect on my personality. Within almost 20 minutes it helps a dormant

part of my mind to start functioning again. It will absolutely change my personality; it connects me with that place where I can be totally on the edge yet never out of control.

Although I enjoy fine wine as an adjunct to a great meal, there's nothing like a nice cold martini at the end of the day. The bar man at the Ritz Hotel in Paris always made the best martinis and I don't know why. Maybe it was the atmosphere. Maybe it was the time of year or the way people were dressed. I gotta tell you it was the best martini I ever had. It was a double, so you knew you were not going to run out too soon. It was cold, because the ice had time to melt while you were drinking. And the olive was there in case you ran out of dinner. In the words of Francis Albert Sinatra, "I'm for anything that gets you through the night whether it's booze or religion." In my life it's been a combination of both. I've been down on my knees drunk and I've been down on my knees praying, and I'm not so sure they weren't at the same time.

Martini

Making a good martini is an art. I think it's the way great chefs prepare a fine dish: It's a combination of elements. You don't necessarily have to go by the book; it's all done by feel. To me, a martini must be made with gin. Not a smooth, mild gin—I like gin with a little bite to it, where you can actually taste the juniper. It also depends on whether you prefer dry or French vermouth. They're totally different. Some people feel that a dry martini means you literally put the vermouth in the glass, pour it out, and then pour in your gin. Actually, it's the meeting of the two when there's just enough of the bite of the juniper and just enough of the fla vor of the vermouth. But if the vermouth or the gin takes over, it destroys the martini. One of my favorite martinis was at the old Chasen's. They burned an orange peel, and the oil from the orange was rubbed onto the glass. I also like to add one drop, a tiny drop on a toothpick, of Pernod.

All the variations aside, what a martini really needs to be is cold. When you're making a martini, much of the secret is in the glass. The glass shouldn't be too thick or the martini won't stay cold. And a martini is best if mixed in a silver shaker, because silver gets so cold that ice forms around it. Then you pour it into a chilled glass and you're off to the races.

I don't remember my first martini at all. And it worked that way with my last martini. I think that's probably why I drink martinis. But any way you figure it, alcohol is strong medicine and should be taken in small doses.

I really don't enjoy drinking alone. I drink to be sociable, because basically I'm a little bit shy, and I can get over the edge of shyness with a drink or two. But alcoholism runs in my family, so it is something I am very aware of. I've always been careful as to exactly how far I can go.

I can't say the same thing when it comes to women. However, I hope my relationships with women have always been a source of mutual pleasure. I love women. Women approach men in many different ways. Some women want to be a man's pal: They play cards with you, drink with you, and watch sports with you. It's nice because in a way they become one of the guys, but such women have to be careful. Being perceived as a buddy is often not the best way to initiate a romantic relationship with a man, because that is how he will treat you. It should be in your bag of tricks, but you really shouldn't lead with it.

Why is it that women are so much smarter than men, except when it comes to men? Many women are stuck being attracted to bad boys. Maybe it's just a phase they have to go through. Women seem to like a little bit of a rake or a cad, probably because these types are more interesting. A bad boy is always a little bit unobtainable; they know a woman's game and know how to play to her blind side, as romantic as that might sound.

It would be great if women would remember one simple thing: Men are like children, and if they would just learn to handle them like children, they would be able to win the game. You need to make a man think that everything is his idea, that he is the one in charge. It then becomes possible to move a man in any direction as long as you always make it seem as though it was his idea to begin with. The whole trick to dealing with a man is to let him win. Men want to win in the eyes of a woman. Smart women know this and use it to their benefit.

Most truly great women are enormously flawed, and that is what is interesting about them. I don't care how strong or important a woman is, they really are very insecure and fragile. Gloria Swanson projected an indomitable image, but she was one of the kindest and most intriguing women I have ever met. She was humorous and interested in other people. When I was a child, I remember Gloria Swanson sitting on the floor of my house in blue jeans talking to me about Joe Kennedy. Merle Oberon was another fascinating woman. She was a mystery and an enigma. She had lost the one true love of her life in a tragic accident, and although she kept company with many men, her heart remained true to that one unrequited love. She inherently understood what was unique in a person and also had the guts to defy the social conventions of Hollywood.

I have yet to meet a woman I can settle down with. I need a lot of peace and quiet to counterbalance the fast pace that my life and business are moving at these days. I need time to be in my own company. If I were a bit older, perhaps, and had the ability to do nothing, I think I would enjoy having a woman in my life to travel with and enjoy the adventure. Basically, women are like a fine violin: They just need to be appreciated and bowed properly. You should find their changes amusing, not annoying.

The old adage "Lucky at cards, unlucky at love" might very well be true in my case. Gambling has always been a pleasure for me. When it comes to luck, I have learned to trust my instincts. It's almost as if I tap into a certain level of energy that is almost hypnotic. It has nothing to do with the odds. I have extraordinary luck, but I also have the guts to play with that luck. I'm dangerous when I get ahead because I'll double up or triple up. When I'm playing with someone else's money, that's the time to get dangerous. Don't get dangerous when you're playing with your own money. The same holds true in life.

Once when I was in England, I had an incredible run at the tables that lasted for 28 nights straight. I walked in with no money in my pocket and a friend loaned me 10,000 pounds. I felt an amazing surge of energy in the casino and decided to play baccarat. Within 15 minutes I had won more than 50,000 pounds. An absolutely gorgeous woman was also at the table, and I asked her to turn the cards for me. With each turn I requested that the table limit be raised. After a few winning hands, a billionaire who was playing next to me looked over at the woman and said, "You are very lucky."

I gave him a look and said, "Of course she's lucky. She's with me."

My philosophy in a casino has always been to hit and run: Push the table stakes higher when you're feeling lucky, and get out the minute the energy changes. Playing for a few brief and productive minutes each night, I managed to walk away with $1,230,000 total.

I've had some wild times gambling. One night when I was in Monte Carlo, I wanted to see how far the casino would go to accommodate me. I told Adnan Khashoggi that my neck was sore, and he introduced me to a chiropractor who was happy to adjust my spine, courtesy of the casino. Not wanting to break my rhythm, I asked if it was possible if they could clear a roulette table so he could work on me, and of course they did. In the middle of the adjustment, I asked the pit boss if my number came up, would I get 35 of me? As you can see, even when I'm at a gambling table I have a hard time taking myself too seriously. Liquor, Ladies, and Luck: When you know what you're doing, they can be three of the greatest little pleasures going.

Life's

Never,
ever take yourself—
or life—
too seriously...

Little

...and always be able
to joke about yourself.

Pleasures

THE PLEASURES
of Defining Your Own Style

When I got to Hollywood, it quickly became clear that the game was really quite simple. It was very easy to get by with a lot of "front" and you didn't need a lot of "back." After all, you can only wear one suit at a time or drive one car at a time or wear one watch at a time. I found that I could look like a millionaire by having all the suggestive accouterments of great wealth. Hollywood is a very interesting spot: People have less to be snobbish about here, yet they are more snobbish than anywhere else in the world.

A certain form of security comes from creating a persona. Once you put it together, that persona can then shield you from many things in life. Creating a persona or an aura is a lot like wearing a hood ornament. It is merely an advertisement about who you are. For years people took me only at face value, and that was all I showed them. Eventually my persona started to take over, and it grew larger than the film roles I was playing. People thought I was not a serious actor because of the persona I projected in real life. I learned that you don't have to be a minority to be stereotyped. I found I was stereotyped as a rich playboy, and for years I played into that stereotype.

Remember: It is not necessarily how you dress; it is how your clothing complements your personality. People really shouldn't be looking at your clothes at all, they should be looking at you. Creating an aura is not about purchasing a designer

f I were a twin, the other one would be exhausted.

label or a custom-tailored suit. It comes from an innate resonation of your personality. It's about walking into a room with a look that says "I'm a player" yet having the sense of humor not to take yourself too seriously.

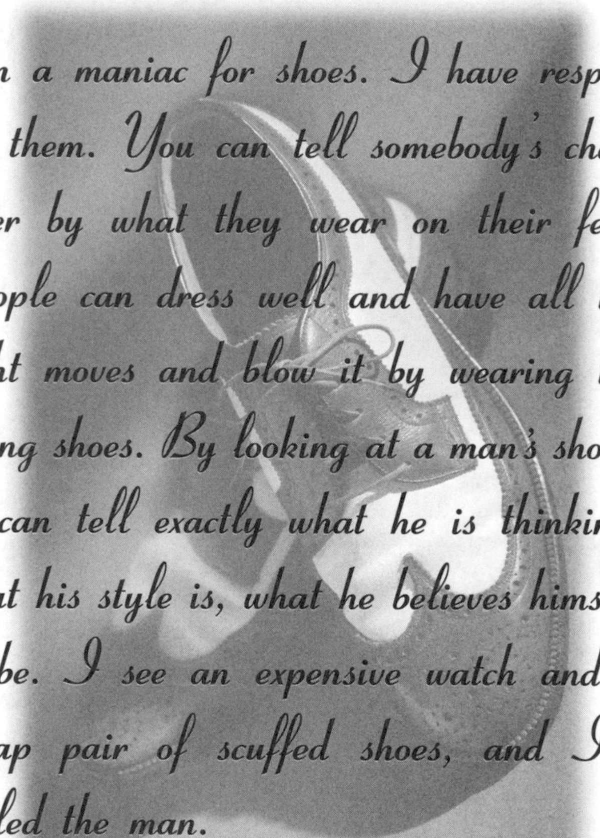

I'm a maniac for shoes. I have respect for them. You can tell somebody's character by what they wear on their feet. People can dress well and have all the right moves and blow it by wearing the wrong shoes. By looking at a man's shoes, I can tell exactly what he is thinking, what his style is, what he believes himself to be. I see an expensive watch and a cheap pair of scuffed shoes, and I've nailed the man.

I never wear the same pair of shoes two days in a row. Every pair I own is meticulously shined and cared for like a work of art. I make sure they're kept in shoe trees, preferably cedar. I used to have an English butler, and he taught me the proper way to shine shoes. You need to start with a clean surface. Use vinegar and water to remove the dirt and the old polish. Once it's cleaned, apply meltonian cream in the appropriate color to get a nice, soft look. Then you buff it off using a brush. There is nothing I love better than for every shoe I own to be perfectly shined.

It's no secret that I also love clothes. They set a mood for me. I can create a place in my head where I want to be simply by what I choose to wear. Perhaps it comes from years of being an actor. The other day it was raining and my wardrobe said, "It's raining. We're in England, old boy." Corduroy pants, boots for the field, plaid shirt, and a riding mack, by George. There I was, perfectly comfortable.

Sometimes style is intangible. I was once in a movie that Dore Schary was producing and he told me, "If you want to look like a million bucks tonight, put five thousand dollars in your pocket right before you go out to do the scene." Well, I put the money in my pocket, and suddenly there was a totally different me than there was before.

You might start out dressing for others, but eventually you will have to dress for yourself. It's not about what you wear—it's about who you are, and eventually you will have to express that. Clothes should lead you toward the people who will identify with you. Then you just might become a classic in your own right.

People often focus too much on having this year's clothes and then getting rid of them next year. Being in step with the latest fashion is the surest way to be out of date. Sure, you can pay homage to everything that is new by knowing about it and letting it creep into your closet, but keep in mind it will soon have to creep out again. There is something to be said about the classics. Alana was once looking at a photo taken in the 1970s of me standing in between Elton John and Rod Stewart. She teased me because I looked so conservative back then, dressed in a business suit with a pocket square and tie. Well, when I look at that photo today, I get a good laugh out of Rod's spandex pants and Elton's Carnaby Street suit—and don't forget those platform shoes. Sometimes you may be in when you're out and you don't even know it. Think about it: Cary Grant and Fred Astaire lived through almost 40 years of film history, and if you look closely, you will see that there really wasn't much change in their wardrobes over the course of their careers.

For women, it's decidedly different. There is nothing more exhausting than trying to teach a young woman how to dress. Really, all you have to do is expose her. I don't mean literally, of course. Just take her around and let her notice other women, and you'll see changes in her that you couldn't make if you had a mallet in your hand. All great women dress for each other. They shop at the same places, and they have an incredibly chic look about them. Everything is understated. They'll juxtapose something inexpensive with something really expensive and yet it is all thought out. Their style expresses who they are in a very subtle way. It's a

To me, everything has
to be a classic and last.

form of Morse code; women send out signals that will be received by the very people that they want to attract.

Many people overlook the pleasure of taking care of themselves. One way to do this is through proper skin care. Since men and women are both short on time, skin care should be easy—a four-step program with products that exfoliate, cleanse, tone, and moisturize. I have put together a no-nonsense regime that follows these steps, and, for men, have added an aftershave and cologne with hints of an attractive masculine scent that sends out signals. While I do sell these products on television, I have been known to deliver door-to-door. My experience in marketing products on TV is that people are trying to find good value in what they buy. That is why, whether I make products for QVC or department stores, I am committed to developing something that is excellent and will last, with a simple, understated perception of style—all for the right price. To me, everything has to be a classic and last.

If you want to be pampered, getting a massage or a facial is always a satisfying way, but don't forget to enjoy the grooming rituals that you might otherwise take for granted. One of my favorite Little Pleasures is going to the barber. I go to Sam Drucker's in Beverly Hills because it is one of the last great barbershops. The haircut there is $25. No hundred-dollar gurus here. Every top guy in the world, from Ronald Reagan to Bugsy Siegel, has gone there at one time or another. Drucker's has barbers who are absolute wizards with a scissors and comb.

It's an art form that has virtually disappeared. Nowadays, if you're lucky enough to find a guy who can shape your head, it's phenomenal. And if you're lucky enough to find a barber who can give you an old-fashioned hot shave, it's nirvana. To me there is a different look you get at a barbershop than the look you get at a beauty salon. The trouble is, most beauty salons just don't understand how a man's hair should be cut.

When I sit down in a barber's chair, I feel like a Ferrari that's come in for service: They're rotating my tires, adjusting the lug nuts, and changing the fenders. I want that kind of speed and attendance, and then I want to get up and leave. The old-fashioned barbershop is the best. That's where you can hear a good joke, get a shot of booze, and enjoy a cigar. There's always a game on, and they have these great old girls there that do the manicures. When a man gets a manicure he doesn't need polish, but his nails should look healthy and shiny. A man should never have his cuticles touched by anyone. Once he starts that, he gets a hangnail

tipping

and it's all over. I think personal hygiene is terribly important, so a proper haircut and groomed fingernails are essential. For about $50 I've had everything done in about 20 minutes. I like to be pampered, but not in a female way. I don't like beauty salons because they make a man feel like a housewife. But when you sit down in a barber's chair and the barber puts a little piece of paper around your neck and dusts you with talcum powder like barbers have been doing for a hundred years, there is just something incredibly civilized about that. It's a masculine form of pampering that is one of life's simple pleasures.

Always make sure you leave a good tip. As a wise man once said, no one ever got rich by undertipping a barber, cocktail waitress, or taxicab driver. I have found even the most sophisticated people haven't a clue about the proper way to tip. The way a person tips is indicative of their personal style, and very few people have mastered this practice. TIP should be an acronym for To Insure Pleasure or To Insure Proper Service. If you're going to lead a pleasurable life, it is important to know how to oil your way around the world. Tipping is a dying art, partly because much of the pleasure has been taken out of the process.

As a young actor, I never knew if I was tipping too much or too little. How does one know what is proper nowadays when it has almost gotten to the point where tipping is automatically included or expected? I find it incredibly nervy that a hotel adds a 17 percent service charge to your bill and then has the temerity to ask for a gratuity. It has become a form of capitalistic communism. The original thought was that if someone did something really nice for you, you wanted to do something nice for them in return. The problem now is the presumption that they have already done the favor for you, and that attitude has taken the pleasure out of tipping. People who really have to work for a living seem to tip the most appropriately. Bartenders and restaurant servers are the best tippers, because they know what it's like to live on tips. In European countries you leave a little change on top of your bill and that's it. America has got this 20 percent thing and sometimes it's just added onto the bill for you. But ultimately, a tip is a sign of mutual respect. Unfortunately people think they must tip or else they are going to look bad. It takes a very gutsy person to say, "I'm not going to tip unless I get great service." People feel intimidated by the whole notion of tipping, and we have got to stop tipping when we do not receive the service that we expect.

If you want to use money to oil your way, the best exposure is up front. Slip the maître d' a 20 when you give him your name. If you're looking for a long-term relationship with a particular restaurant, though, the best way to tip is on the back end. If you've given them a lot of money up front, they might give you the best table for the nouveau riche, not the best table for the Old Guard. It is important to know which table is which, because too many people are willing to spend any amount of money to sit in the wrong spot. I always fold whatever I'm going to tip into a small square. I never show it and I never make a point of pulling the money out of my pocket. I keep it between my fingers and when I shake the maître d's hand, I leave it in his hand. Tipping should be absolutely underplayed.

To me, $20 is an adequate amount; $50 should suffice in a place that is hard to get in to; and if you have to tip $100, you don't deserve to be there.

So now you're dressed, your shoes are shined, you're well coifed, and you have the confidence that comes from understanding the pleasures of slipping someone a tip. But there is still something missing, one of Life's Little Pleasures that I learned early on. An essential element of my style is my tan.

My love affair with the sun began in Galveston, Texas, when I was seven years old. It was the first time I had experienced the intoxicating effect of combining salt water and the sun. Growing up, I really never thought much about suntans, except to associate them with movie stars. Those were the good old days, an era when no one worried about the dangers of smoking, drinking, or suntanning, and everyone seemed to have a good time. Now people worry about everything. Have you ever noticed that pale fellow in the black suit at every board meeting, obsessing over his calorie intake and cholesterol count? I'm convinced he's the one who's taking heroin.

When I was going to prep schools in New York I always had the most godawful pallor. I'd look at pictures of Florida during spring break, and I'd think to myself, *If I ever got down there, I'd go to the beach.* I was kind of a nerd and the class clown in prep school. While I got all the laughs, I usually never got the girl. I just wasn't particularly attractive to women. One spring break, I finally went to Florida and hit the beach, thus beginning my lifelong love affair with the sun. The tanner I got, the more girls found me attractive. I couldn't understand the change, but I wasn't about to argue with the results. My teeth were whiter and my eyes were brighter, but more than that, I felt better with a tan. Luckily, the sun has always been kind to me and I have never had a skin problem.

After I got to Hollywood, Bob Mitchum, Cary Grant, and Glenn Ford taught me that if I had a good tan, I wouldn't have to wear much makeup. We would spend our lunch hours lying outside with our little sun reflectors, soaking up enough rays to make us look better on camera. Years later, we started to hear about the dangers of too much sun, so one day I tried a tanning product called Man Tan. I turned bright orange and smelled like a toxic waste dump. Eventually, I developed a line of products that include an instant tanning cream as well as an auto bronzer to keep me from having to spend too much time in the sun. Both products have a fabulous apricot scent and will make you look as if you have spent hours in the sun. I put them on daily and people have never said anything negative to me about the way I look.

There is nothing like a good tan to make you feel wealthy and healthy. To this day, anytime I smell suntan lotion I am transported to an entirely different place. Remember, the secret lies in taking pleasures in the little things.

Life's

A hand-rolled Cuban cigar and a glass of very old port…

Littl

…shared with your
son while you
talk about life.

Pleasures

The Only Job You Can't Be Fired From

The Pleasures of Parenthood

I learned about the pleasures of parenting fairly late in my career. Fortunately, I learned about them before it was too late. When Ashley was a young child, I was working most of the time. Later, when my marriage to Alana dissolved, I was relegated to the role of weekend father. To Alana's credit, we kept the lines of communication open and adhered to similar values in both our homes. It wasn't the ideal situation, but at least Ashley was never able to play one parent off the other. Like most parents who divorce, Alana and I had a fair amount of guilt, but we tried never to allow the guilt to overwhelm our better judgment when it came to raising Ashley.

Unfortunately, children—those adorable little bundles—don't come with an instruction book. The pleasures of parenthood are derived mostly from on-the-job training. It's important to understand that in any given situation, you're going to do the best you can with the tools you have available at the time. A father has less knowledge about how to handle a child than a mother does. Women have the most amazing ability to create these fascinating creatures. Forget about penis envy; I really think that men envy women because they are actually able to create children. Women are far superior to men because they can give birth to something and men can't.

Life's little pleasures are many. On the other hand, life's great pleasures are few. Having a son like Ashley is one of the greatest.

Men have the ability to lead by example. If we can live our lives a certain way, our example becomes the most important asset we can give our children. If we try to preach to them but not live by our own word, they see us as old patronizing fools. I feel most of the instruction that a child needs comes at the beginning of their lives. For the first three years, they need to be held and touched more than anything else, and love is the order of the day. Women need to love them and hold them, and then learn to let them go. And that is a hard lesson for many women to learn. If you don't let a child go, you weaken them by holding on to them. Fathers have the innate instinct to show their little birds how to fly out of the nest. It's upsetting to women, but it is the basis of the whole circle of parenthood.

Basically, whether it is early in life through the sense of touch, or later in life by setting limits, children need well-defined boundaries. Fathers don't have the same tactile input as mothers do. Although he certainly shares the duties of parenthood, his major contribution to the child's upbringing comes later. A child emulates the father, and a father can give a child the benefit of his experience. A child also learns a great deal from watching the way the father relates to the mother. Never say bad things about the other parent. The child inherently feels that he or she is half the mother and half the father, and if you denigrate one parent, the child will feel bad about him- or herself.

My parents divorced when I was quite young, and I grew up with a series of stepfathers. Later, as a young man, I sought out my father, the bandleader "Spike"

My dad used to tell me there were three kinds of men in the world, and they could be compared to the calibers of handguns—.22s, .38s, and .45s. He hoped I'd grow up to be a .45. One way or another, I knew I'd be a son of a gun.

Hamilton, and got to know him. He really didn't know how to relate to me. It was through the sharing of his stories about being a musician and bonding over a pipe or cigar that we came to know each other. Over drinks and cigars I learned about his philosophy of life. And that history has repeated itself in my relationship with Ashley.

We were in England together one Thanksgiving when Ashley was about 17. It was "my turn" to spend the holiday with him, but he just wanted to be back in the States with his friends. Who could blame him? For that matter, Thanksgiving is not something they really celebrate in England. Ashley was fairly sullen about the whole mess. No friends, no turkey, and being forced to spend time with his father.

Not a great combination any way you look at it. So I searched all over London and convinced the Connaught Grill to cook a turkey for us. This only depressed Ash further, having to sit in this stodgy English grill when all he wanted was stuffing and gravy and his mother's black-eyed peas. When they rolled this turkey out on a silver trolley, it was just a disaster.

After dinner they came over and offered us a glass of port, and I suddenly remembered my father and all of those awkward dinners we had growing up, so for the first time in Ashley's life I offered him a cigar. They brought over a beautiful humidor, and I taught him how to choose a cigar and the proper way to smoke it. When we shared that cigar, it was a bonding experience. It was wonderful to see how my father and I had passed a tradition on to my son. A sense of personal history was being played out. I felt a closeness with Ash that I had not shared with another human being since my own father had died.

The pleasure of seeing your children turn out well is one of the greatest joys in the world. At whatever point that happens, young or old, you get a sense of the amazing contribution that you have made to their lives, and they to yours. One of the pleasures of being the parent of a grown child is realizing that she or he really is an extension of you. You want to save your child the pain of going through the hard lessons that you went through. Some children are born with shortcuts in their lives and some have to go through their own set of mistakes to learn the lessons. But they get there one way or another. And they remember everything. It's amazing that you can be with them for the rest of their lives whether you are physically with them or not.

So many people try to be "friends" with their children, and I think that shortchanges both parties. You have to be the parent first. You have to do things that your children aren't necessarily going to like, but you need to have their respect. If you don't have their respect, having their friendship really means very little. You want your children to understand the consequences of their actions and what it means to be an adult. You want them to enjoy their childhood but also understand the responsibilities of adulthood. Children need to learn how to get a job, save money, and build a structure to their lives. Quite often it's hard to teach those lessons and be their friend at the same time. But if you have their respect, and they come to you for advice, it's wonderful.

If, God forbid, there is a defect in your child, sometimes it is apparent and sometimes it is not. I think that children who are born with challenges are incredible gifts to their families and to the world. Part of being a parent is starting from scratch—remember, there is no how-to manual—and giving your children as much as you can to ensure that they reach their capacity, whatever that may be. With Ashley, we as a family had to deal with his addiction, and it was an amazing experience for all of us. Fortunately for us, Ashley survived some pretty perilous times. When you possess the genetic predisposition to alcoholism or drug addiction, there is the possibility that you can have three children brought up in the same

It used to drive us bats figuring out a Halloween costume for Ashley until I did the vampire comedy farce, Love at First Bite. *This Dracula costume was good for at least a couple of reruns.*

family, the same way, and only one will develop the disease. Addiction is a disease, and it is to be treated as one. It doesn't mean that as a parent you don't feel guilt; you feel a tremendous amount of guilt. You feel that your child's addiction is somehow your fault.

As a parent, I had to learn to deal with addiction as well so we could deal with it effectively as a family. Addiction is absolutely devastating. It brings you together and separates you at the same time. To have a successful recovery, you have to work through all the issues surrounding the addiction. People who have the support of their family and have learned not to blame them or themselves are usually more successful at recovering than those who don't. Being supportive is one of the most important ways that you can contribute to your child's recovery. Show them that you care and that there is solidarity. Fortunately, we were able to share as a family one of the rare pleasures of parenthood: seeing one's child get well.

One of the things I learned in Ashley's recovery, through attending family therapy, is that the brain of the addict is controlled by the alcohol or the drug to the point where they don't have the ability to cut off or monitor themselves at all. They are often in total denial right up until they go into rehabilitation. When you're talking to them, you're really talking to the alcohol or the drug. Once you learn that and stop beating up on them and on yourself, you can start making progress. This can lead to one of the closest and most intimate family relationships you could ever hope to have. Parenting is hard enough, but when you add in addiction, you have to grow up along with your child. Part of it is letting go and not being judgmental yet knowing that you have to be vigilant at the same time. There are wonderful treatment centers today, and Alcoholics Anonymous is a terrific program. AA is one of the few places in the world where people can have real conversations with one another. Rich or poor, black or white, everyone tells the same story. You used to feel you're special, but you're not. And no matter what happens in your life, you can't beat yourself up. You just have to move on.

In spite of whatever I did or didn't do as a father while Ashley was growing up, I am lucky enough to have the pleasure of enjoying moments with my grown son as an equal. We share the bond of father and son, and now we also share our interests, passions, and adventures. Surprisingly, I can think of no greater pleasure on Earth than spending time with my son.

Life's

Downshifting in a Ferrari...

Littl

...going 80 mph in an Italian tunnel.

Pleasures

The Pleasures of Being a Good Host...

and a Gracious Guest

Whether you're going to them or giving them, parties are stressful. But whereas some people are natural-born hosts, I am a natural-born guest. Few people really understand how to make others feel at ease. Haven't you ever noticed a harried hostess who talks distractedly to you as she looks over your shoulder to see who is at the door? Conversely, one of the worst things a guest can do is to monopolize the time and energy of the host. You should exchange a few words, kiss the host on both sides of the cheek, and do what you really want to do: Go get a drink.

Invariably, well-meaning hosts try to mix the interesting people in with the boring people. I've always felt that all the boring people should sit together at one table. It just doesn't seem fair to get all dressed up and go through all that work of preparing for and getting to a party, only to realize that you just might be the most interesting person at the table. It should be like it was at school: The brightest children should be put together so they can grow the fastest, and the slower learners should sit in the corner.

Even though my grandmother taught me never to show up at a person's home empty-handed, I'm not overly fond of bringing the hostess a gift. Certainly a well-chosen wine or a box of expensive chocolates is thoughtful, but it may make

With some women you are lucky to hold your own. When you enter a room with Joan Collins on your arm she literally lights up the place. Some of my best suntans have come from the lights of the flash cameras bouncing off her lovely skin.

other nonbearing guests feel uncomfortable. I always like to send my hostess a beautiful arrangement of flowers and a lovely thank-you note the day after the party, acknowledging what a wonderful evening it was. If you do that, you will be well remembered and certain to be invited to the next gathering.

Part of being a gracious guest is to try to remember to circulate. Move as quickly as possible. Be stealthy. Try to meet as many people as possible. Keep the conversation light. There is nothing worse than someone discussing Proust or their latest root canal at a cocktail party. With any luck, you'll meet the attractive stranger who captures your imagination and then switch place cards so you can sit next to him or her at dinner.

The main component of being a good host is that you must be at ease, or at least seem to be. It's all about good planning. Being a good host is a lot like being the conductor of an orchestra. All it involves is being familiar with what people do, and never allowing too many people in the same line of business to be in the same room at the same time.

Try to know enough about the people you have invited so that you can immediately cross-reference them to somebody else. It's also a good idea to be aware of people's body language. When you see a guest who is not talking or who is backing away from the action, walk up to her and say, "There's somebody who wants to meet you." Bringing people together is easier than you think. Pick two people who don't know each other. Approach each one individually and say, "You know, there's a girl/guy here who asked about you earlier." They will find each other the most charming person in the whole place, and they won't even know they've been set up. They just think they've been approved of.

Another secret to being a good hostess is to look like you're enjoying the party as much as your guests are. A good party is quite theatrical and actually is no different from making a movie. The minute a guest walks in the door, I get him a drink. If someone makes the terrible mistake of asking you for a drink that involves a blender or anything with an umbrella in it, you should smile and ask her if she wouldn't mind putting on a uniform and going to work.

Nowadays in Hollywood, people go to parties based only on what food is being served and who is coming to dinner. They will ask you about this up front. And as soon as dinner is served, they run right home. I guess a lot of people in Hollywood have been hungry in earlier parts of their lives, and they want to be sure a decent meal is being served. New York parties are totally different from Hollywood parties. Besides the fact that most people on The Right Coast can conjugate verbs, New York parties have lots of wonderful hors d'oeuvres and terrific drinks, but they're not very big on dinner. In Hollywood it's skip the appetizers, forget the drinks, let's hurry up and have dinner because I gotta get home to read a script and be at the studio by seven-thirty. Or, I'm suing the studio at seven-thirty. Or, my client is filing bankruptcy at seven-thirty. It's a terrible thing to put in all that time and effort when it's ultimately not appreciated because your guests have to leave as soon as the soufflé tombes. You practically have to lock people in the dining room and force them to have a good time. Furthermore, few in Hollywood really know how to carry on a conversation that doesn't start with "I" or "me," or involve negotiations over film rights, or include the word *points.*

One night, the esteemed agent Swifty Lazar said to me, "I'd love to come to your dinner party, but I have to leave at ten-thirty."

"Why?" I asked.

"Because I have to be up at six-thirty," he said.

"Why?" I asked again, incredulous.

"It's what I do every day of my life," he replied.

"Well, then," I offered, "isn't it time for a change?"

He thought for a moment. "No," he answered, "I'm leaving at ten-thirty regardless." So I had the doors locked until midnight. Swifty later admitted to me that he had never enjoyed himself so much at a party. He was forced to dance and meet other people and not hide in the corner and make book deals with Ronald Reagan.

One of the secrets to hosting a great party is to make sure that there is just enough time for drinks and not to allow the cocktail hour to drag on to the point where your guests are too drunk to enjoy dinner. It's horrible when your dinner is transformed into the process of sobering up. Serve two drinks in fairly short succession, and then dinner should be served. You want to get those two drinks into your guests as quickly as possible, because alcohol is the key to loosening everybody up. Rosalind Russell was a wizard at this. The minute you walked into her home, you were handed a shot of Aquavit, which was served in a glass with a round bottom so you couldn't set it down. As soon as you finished your first drink, a second was poured. In their nervousness, the guests had absolutely no idea what was going on. After two quick shots of Aquavit, people were making promises for five-picture deals, proposing marriage to their stockbrokers...but one thing is for sure: Everyone enjoyed themselves. Knowing how to combine food and booze is as essential as the host enjoying himself, even if it's an act.

The pleasure of being a good host or hostess means that although you have a sense of responsibility that your guests don't, it is a joy to know that you have truly given something. Life is nothing but reciprocating, and soon it will be time for your guest to become your host. And if you're a good host, you will invariably be invited to become a guest.

Life's

Walking into a gothic cathedral,

lighting a

Littl

candle...

and infusing your prayers into the flame.

Pleasures

Unplug and Disconnect Without Going Crazy

The Pleasures of Solitude

I really enjoy spending time alone, and I find that these days I just don't get enough of it. I have a hard time understanding people who can't enjoy the pleasure of their own company. I have a friend who is quite successful in life and is absolutely petrified at the prospect of spending time by himself. It's almost as if being alone with his thoughts is like being in a bad neighborhood. He is constantly in need of stimulation: gambling, women, drinking, buying the latest toys. He is always rushing off to work or to the club or to the gym. Come to think of it, it sounds like the way most people think I live my life.

I find it emotionally draining to spend any time with this friend socially. When I asked him the other day why he doesn't spend time in solitude, he looked at me incredulously and said, "Why would I want to spend time alone? I like people. Alone? How boring." I offered that only boring people get bored. This message was completely lost on him.

So much of my life is spent either in the collaborative art of moviemaking or in working with people to build my cigar and nightclub business that I need my alone time to recharge my batteries. The ability to enjoy hours of solitude is an important attribute to leading a pleasurable life.

As a young MGM studio player I was given all kinds of lessons—dancing lessons, fencing lessons, horse riding lessons. It was the studio's way of preparing me for any role they decided to throw my way. Right after I learned to ride and perfect the quick draw, they put me in a beach epic called Where the Boys Are. Go figure.

This is a picture of me as a young soldier in the epic war film, The Victors. *The poignant wintertime scene when Private Slovac was executed by a firing squad to the tune of "Have Yourself a Merry Little Christmas" caused some moviegoers to leave the theater in protest. To tell you the truth, by the time this long, grueling movie was through shooting, Private Slovac wasn't the only one who was willing to risk a firing squad to go home.*

There are many ways to make your time alone a chance to get reacquainted with yourself. I love to read. I have found that books can become great friends. One of my favorite things in the world is to go into a bookstore on a Saturday night and buy 20 books and bring them home and put them in bed with me. Then I read three or four pages at a time of each book and change books whenever I want to change my mood. I'm always trying to improve myself, so I like to read books on business. I also enjoy biographies and books on health and spirituality. I've never really enjoyed reading fiction. Life, in my opinion, is so bizarre that I can't figure out why anyone would want to make up a story to read. Real life is so much more fascinating.

I also like to putter. Military school taught me the importance of self-reliance and order. There is nothing quite like having your life in perfect order. It is basically an outward representation of the inward structure of your mind—if you have order around you, your mind will be in order. Whenever I get into a situation in which I feel overwhelmed, I clean out my sock drawer or organize my closets. I like to give things away. It feels great. Not only does it get rid of clutter, but it also creates the space, emotionally and physically, for new stuff. You'd be surprised how much you can pare your life down if you really want to.

To be able to unplug is to be able to let go of all the material things that you feel support you. It's ego—admittedly, you're not your car. Having said that, I have never quite gotten over the need for an important car. I don't like mere transportation; I like to ride in style. Car manufacturers nowadays have taken out the burled wood and put in more plastic and the price has gone up, but I haven't lost my taste for the classics. I have a weakness for a well-made automobile. I really love Bentleys because they have all the luxury without sacrificing performance. It's one of the luxuries I have always afforded myself even when I couldn't afford it. And I love to pack a few CDs or even some books on tape and take a leisurely drive up the coast to spend an afternoon walking on the beach alone.

Although I travel a great deal on business, I enjoy traveling alone. There is no one else's schedule to take into account. You can experience what you want, at the pace you want. When I used to be able to travel anonymously, it was an excellent way to make new friends. How often would you strike up a conversation with a total stranger if you were traveling with someone else? Some people are

relax

intimidated by the idea of dining out alone. But I have found that you can walk into just about any restaurant in the world with a book in your hand and sit down and enjoy a meal solo. It's amusing to make up stories in your head about your fellow diners, too. If you've done it a few times, it actually comes quite naturally. The same goes for the theater or the symphony or a museum. Plus, you never know whom you're going to meet. Remember, it's always better to be alone than in bad company. There is absolutely nothing worse than being in the right place with the wrong person.

Some of the best mini-vacations I've had have involved checking into a hotel in my own city. I put out the *DO NOT DISTURB* sign and live on 24-hour room service. This nirvana can go on only for so long, however. Invariably, after two days there's a knock on your door because the front desk is worried that you have committed suicide. You have to call them and tell them that *DO NOT DISTURB* means that even if there is a fire in the hotel, it is optional whether or not they should call you.

Sleep is one of the greatest pleasures of all. Turn off the phone, close the blinds, and tune out the world for a few days. Sleep is a great escape for me. Until recently, I didn't really know how to just let go and relax. I always felt like time was running out and I always had to be doing something. But lately I have learned that I don't have to keep busy all the time. I just have to be. I used to go until I was ragged. Now, I'm a great napper. I have also learned to meditate.

Meditate

Nothing refreshes me more than 20 minutes spent in total silence with my eyes closed. Meditation can be one of the best stress reducers around, and there are many books and classes on different ways to meditate.

Some people really enjoy the Internet and being online. While e-mail is a great way to keep in touch, I have become concerned that we have replaced conversation with chatting on-line. It's an efficient means of connecting when you are in a rush, and an inexpensive way of staying in touch with your children when they are away at college, but it can also be quite addictive. The wife of a friend of mine has spent so many hours playing bingo on the Internet and cruising the chat rooms that it has ruined their sex life. The World Wide Web indeed serves many vital purposes, but there is also a Whole Wide World out there to experience in person. It's fun to spend an hour here or there surfing the Net, but I don't think it's a good idea to spend your life relating to your computer.

I also think television is absolutely wonderful in small doses and one of the worst things in the world as a constant companion. Sadly, a lot of people have replaced conversations in their lives with The Tube. Still, you can get a good education from the television. Watch a little CNN, A&E, the Discovery Channel, or PBS. I can't get enough of Charlie Rose, and the Two Fat Ladies' cooking show always makes me laugh. To rinse my brain out, I like to tune into *American Justice* and *Cops*. I really don't understand sitcoms, although I've been on quite a few of them. (I'm sure there are people out there who can't believe I was on them, either.)

I've been fortunate enough to experience the joys of solitude on many occasions. Solitude doesn't mean being in solitary, nor does it mean just being alone. Solitude is an area in your soul that you can retreat to when everything goes wrong. It is a place of quiet and reflection where you can experience a sense of deep pleasure. Initially, it can be a hard place to find, but once you find it you can return to it often. It's like looking through a keyhole into another room. During the 1960s I suppose a lot of people dropped acid when it was in vogue to see glimpses of that other side. Some reached it, some never came back from the journey, and some actually came back better people. I've never taken the drug, but I have had momentary glimpses when I felt I had entered the part of my soul that unites me with everyone and everything in the world.

Solitude comes easiest when I'm next to something bigger than I am, like a mountain or the ocean. I am awed by nature and its stillness and all of my self-importance goes out the window. I'm left alone with a sense of peace, and after my brain stops churning I notice that my breathing changes. I realize that I am taking deeper breaths and my thoughts are slowing down. I'm no longer worried about what is attacking me from behind or what I might need to accomplish tomorrow. I am aware that I am fully present in the moment. When I meditate, in moments when I am half asleep and half awake, I have that stillness. It's almost like a dream state. Whatever it is, it's better than any drug. Whenever I'm in situations where I feel stressed, I stop for a few minutes, focus on my breathing, and find that I start to think differently. That feeling of solitude gets me centered and everything becomes positive for me. What was stressful no longer is, and energy starts to flow through me. Think of it as a spiritual G spot.

Everyone wants to know how, after all these years of sitting in the sun, my skin can still be so young. Well, here's my secret: I sit in the sun fully clothed. Afterward I go inside and put on my own brand of sun-bronzer.

Some Closing Thoughts

The mind creates a place of pleasure, and if you can just get out of your own way, you can let it take you there. Once you have learned the art of creating pleasure in your life and have practiced it the same way you would perfect your golf swing, you will find that being able to return to that state of mind becomes automatic. Tough concept, isn't it?

Pleasure is all about the way you look at things. If you look at life in an affirmative way, you can immediately change your negative state of mind to a more positive one. We all know that our thoughts can be enormously powerful. The good news is that that power is far greater than we even know. Just as the sand and the rocks and the water are defined by what constantly rolls over them, you're defined by the challenges you have encountered in your life. One door closes and another opens. All of a sudden what you might have been afraid of is no longer to be feared. Certain things lose their importance or their power over you once you've worked through them.

Leading a pleasurable life is about making those small adjustments that can create a huge change in your outlook. It's about feeling entitled to beauty simply because you are alive, and living each moment to the hilt because you get only one shot at it. It's about looking for the gift in the adversity you must deal with, and being able to transcend your circumstances. Believe me, it's much harder to transcend good times than bad ones. I've never been as good as my best reviews, nor as bad as my worst.

Ultimately, pleasure is about being truly present in the moment. When you are in touch with what pleases you, you will know how to take yourself away from worrying about what the future will bring, or obsessing about the mistakes you have made in the past. When you live entirely in the present, you can't help but have true peace of mind. I really think this is a learned behavior. Once you get in the habit of doing it, though, your mind will begin to drift to a place of pleasure quite naturally.

My father once said that it is impossible to keep happiness forever, but you can envelop yourself with beauty all of your life. Surrounding my eyes with beauty is something I am constantly trying to do. So stop waiting for something good to happen—go out and make it happen instead. Buy yourself that present that you long for someone else to give you. Take yourself on that big adventure. Fill your home with objects that are pleasing to you. Treat yourself the way you have always wanted someone else to treat you. After all, if you don't love yourself, there is no way that anybody else is ever going to love you.

I think a passion for life upholds you in a certain way, and I think humor allows you a certain detachment to look at your life as the grand theater that it is. It's having the expectation that when you get out of bed every morning, something incredible is about to happen. Joy is not something that happens by accident of birth, or by the balance in your checkbook, or by waking up with a supermodel in your bed. Joy is something you must consistently seek out and create for yourself. It is not bestowed on you; you must evoke it within yourself. And when you lead a joyful life, you attract more joy. Once you learn that little secret, all of life becomes pretty easy—and a whole lot more fun.

Acknowledgments

I've in no way tried to write my life story or even give much of a hint of what really happened over these 58 years. Instead, I hope you'll look at these essays as an insight into my world part one—a little humor, a little depth, and perhaps the whole story to follow some day.

I am deeply appreciative to Alysse for being me and entering my head while sometimes I was out of it. To Dad for the light in my path; to Mom for the stars that lit my sky; to my brother, Bill, who literally hung the moon; and to my brother, David, who generously shared the early days. To Alana and Ashley, who brought the first sunshine into my darkness, and finally to Peggy, who has been there day and night through all these years, and probably knows the story better than I do.

I love you all.

George

Alysse wishes to gratefully acknowledge...

George Hamilton...for the wonderful opportunity, for all the hours of joy. Creating this book with you was truly a Pleasure.

C.D.B. Bryan...My favorite anachronism, Literary Lion, and a true, dear friend. Thank you for not allowing me to give up on my dream.

David Hirshey...For being the first editor to laugh at my words (in all of the appropriate places), for steadfastly believing in me and for always encouraging the growth of my 'voice.' You are not only loved, you are worth waiting for.

Mike Farrell...Who not only has a great sense of humor, but also knows more about Pleasure than most people give him credit for.

The Carols: Carol "I Can't Read This Chapter After a Glass of Champagne!" Lefko and Carol "What Was That Title?" Riker...for their unflinching support in the face of gourmet food, laughter-filled evenings with George, and copious amounts of exquisite wine. Tough Duty for The Big Bad Broads Club, but we survived.

Shelley Goldberg...Bermuda to Guilford. Chasing after Movie Stars and would-be Feral Cats. Thank you for the Best Guestroom in New York City.

The Pleasure Disciples...Mimi McCormick, Henry Glowa, Helaine Head, and Norm Freed. Thanks for keeping us focused.

The Men: Bruce Alexander, Robert Chefitz, Pat O'Brien, and Ty Griesenbeck... Thank you for living in different time zones. For Houston. Patience and forbearance. Long slow dances. Always returning my phone calls.

The Kaplan-Zuckerman family, the Avedesian family, the Rowe family, Leah Schneider, and Marilyn Nelson for teaching me how it's done.

Mimi Peak, Dr. Tom Dakoske, and Dr. Tiana Shiver...I wouldn't be here without you.

Vicki St George...for her deft (and swift) editorial touch.

Mike Hamilburg...for being the Sweetest Little Pit Bull in Town.

Peter Hoffman...we still haven't had Dinner.

Terence Fagan, Gordon Mott, Marvin Shanken, and the Gang at *Cigar Aficionado*...for always making my "Day Job" a Pleasure.

My assorted and inspiring friends who have tolerated me, edited me, and provided me with great material...Thank you all for reminding me hourly that I am loved.

And finally, to my Mother, Donna Minkoff, who has always taught me everything I ever needed to know about Life's Little Pleasures.